2

1

or
ad
las
pen

METHUEN'S MONOGRAPHS
ON BIOLOGICAL SUBJECTS

General Editor: KENNETH MELLANBY, C.B.E.

THE GENETIC ANALYSIS
OF BEHAVIOUR

The Genetic Analysis of Behaviour

P. A. PARSONS

Professor of Biology
La Trobe University
Melbourne

METHUEN & CO LTD
11 NEW FETTER LANE LONDON EC4

Contents

Preface | *page* vii

Acknowledgements | ix

1 **Introduction** | 1

2 **Single Genes, Inversions, and Behaviour** | 6
2.1 Introduction
2.2 The mating behaviour of yellow and wild type in *Drosophila melanogaster* | 7
2.3 Polymorphisms and inversions in *Drosophila* | 11
2.4 Inversion sequences and mating behaviour in *Drosophila* | 15
2.5 Industrial melanism and mimicry | 22
2.6 Conclusions | 25

3 **Quantitative Traits** | 26
3.1 The nature of continuous variation
3.2 Phenotypic and genotypic values | 30
3.3 Variability of quantitative traits within and between inbred strains | 31
3.4 The components of the genotypic variance | 36
3.5 Crosses between two inbred strains | 38
3.6 Diallel crosses | 43
3.7 Relationships between relatives | 52
3.8 Conclusions | 55

4 **Selection Experiments** | 57
4.1 Introduction
4.2 Defecation and ambulation scores in rats | 60
4.3 Selection experiments in *Drosophila* | 64
4.4 Further possibilities for genetic analysis | 70

5 **The Evolutionary Consequences of Variations in Mating Behaviour**   77
  5.1 Introduction
  5.2 Experimental approach   79
  5.3 Measures of sexual isolation   83
  5.4 Single genes and sexual isolation   86
  5.5 Mating success within and between strains   89
  5.6 Mating success between species   93
  5.7 Modification and evolution of sexual isolation in laboratory populations   95
  5.8 Conclusions   101

6 **Genotype and Behaviour in Rodents**   103
  6.1 Introduction
  6.2 Quantitative traits   104
  6.3 Behavioural traits with a biochemical basis   113
  6.4 Conclusions   120

7 **Behaviour in Man**   122
  7.1 Introduction
  7.2 Behavioural traits due to karyotype abnormalities   123
  7.3 Behavioural traits largely controlled by one gene   125
  7.4 The inheritance of quantitative traits   132
  7.5 Mental illness   137
  7.6 Intelligence and personality traits   141
  7.7 Sense perception   145
  7.8 Assortative mating   148
  7.9 Conclusions   151

8 **Behaviour and Evolution**   153
  References   159
  Index   169

Preface

In recent years there has been growing interest in the role of the genotype in the control of behavioural traits, which has led to a branch of science linking animal behaviour and genetics. This is called behaviour genetics by many people, while others use the term psychogenetics. The term behaviour genetics is probably used more often, and has a wider meaning than psychogenetics, so this will be the term used in this monograph. Although there has been sporadic work in behaviour genetics for many years, often arising as a by-product of other investigations, the first comprehensive text in the field was a book by Fuller and Thompson entitled *Behaviour Genetics*, published in 1960. The time now seems appropriate for a shorter book discussing how a behavioural trait can be analysed from the genetic point of view, with some emphasis on the evolutionary implications of variations in behaviour. The present monograph provides such an attempt. No attempt is made to be exhaustive so far as citing evidence is concerned, as this would be a task beyond the scope of this monograph. Furthermore, the organisms discussed are mainly those with which I have some familiarity. There is a chapter on behaviour in man near the end of the monograph. It is felt that approaching behaviour in man through a knowledge of studies in experimental animals, as has been attempted in this monograph, may help to highlight some of the difficulties in studying the genetic control of behaviour in man.

It is my impression that there is a field of very great interest for those investigators who decide to explore the relationship between genes and behaviour. It is hoped that this monograph may be of some help in indicating both the nature of problems that can be attacked, and some of the methods that are available.

A knowledge of genetics as given in an elementary biology course is assumed, but principles taken from the fields of population and biometrical genetics are explained briefly. Similarly, an elementary level of statistics is assumed, particularly of the analysis of variance, correlation, and regression, but large sections of the book can be read without this knowledge.

I should like to thank Professor M. J. D. White, F.R.S., for facilities enjoyed in his laboratory at the University of Melbourne, and Professor D. G. Catcheside, F.R.S., of the Australian National University for his encouragement and for introducing me to the science of genetics. I would also like to acknowledge helpful discussions with various colleagues and graduate students in the University of Melbourne, in particular Miss Astrid Fleiss, Miss Sally Hosgood, and Mr Ian MacBean. Part of the work for the monograph was carried out during late 1965 to early 1966 while I held a Rockefeller Foundation Travel Grant.

Acknowledgements

The author's and publisher's thanks are due to the following for permission to reproduce or adapt figures: M. Bastock and *Evolution* (Fig. 2.1); E. B. Spiess and B. Langer and *Evolution* (Fig. 2.2); E. B. Spiess and B. Langer and the National Academy of Sciences (U.S.) (Fig. 2.3); C. A. Villee and W. B. Saunders Company (Fig. 3.1); P. L. Broadhurst and H. J. Eysenck and Routledge & Kegan Paul Ltd. (Figs. 4.2 and 4.3); J. Hirsch and *Science* (Figs. 4.4 and 4.5); A. Manning and *Animal Behaviour* (Fig. 4.6); J. M. Thoday and *Nature* (Fig. 4.7); L. Ehrman and *Evolution* (Fig. 5.1); P. L. Broadhurst and J. L. Jinks and the American Genetics Association (Fig. 6.1); G. E. McClearn, E. L. Bennett, M. Hebert, R. Kakihana, and K. Schlesinger, and *Nature* (Fig. 6.2); J. V. Neel and W. J. Schull and University of Chicago Press (Fig. 7.1); R. Fischer, F. Griffin, S. England, and S. M. Garn, and *Nature* (Fig. 7.2).

Fuller details of publications will be found in the References on p. 159.

CHAPTER ONE

Introduction

All people are genetically unique (Medawar, 1965), as is clear when considering the number of segregating systems now known in human populations. Monozygotic twins provide the only exception, since they are derived from the same zygote and so have identical gene complements.

Many segregating systems have their primary manifestation at the biochemical level. Thus it is not difficult to see that genetic individuality implies biochemical individuality. Williams (1956) was one of the first to stress the enormous variations between individuals for biochemical, physiological, and morphological traits, and argued that much of the observed variation was genetic. He argued that the outward individuality of people has a genetic basis, although some of the variability may be environmental. As soon as the environment becomes a factor to be contended with, we face the situation where the primary effects of genes controlling a trait become less discrete and the trait becomes quantitative. The same may happen when gene products interact as must inevitably occur. Furthermore, the environment may affect the type and nature of interactions occasionally leading to large sources of variability due to interactions between genotype and environment.

One can argue that genetic individuality implies behavioural individuality, although there is far less evidence for this than for the link between genetic and biochemical individuality. Although a few behavioural traits are fairly directly under the control of single genes, they are generally more remote from the primary gene products than biochemical traits. This permits further interference by environmental factors and additional interactions between gene products (see Fig. 1.1). Thus many behavioural traits are quantitative in nature without clear-cut segregation into discrete classes, so the experimental designs and methods of analysis of biometrical genetics must be used for their study. Furthermore, since many behavioural traits are quantitative rather than qualitative, some form of completely objective measurement must be used in their study. Even if only marginally subjective, a measurement will be subject to error and hence misinterpretation when it comes to assessing the relative importance of

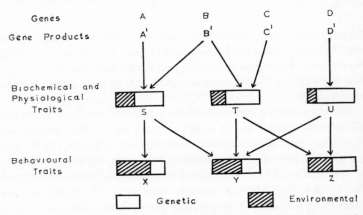

FIG. I.I Schematic representation of the path from genes to biochemical and physiological traits, and then to behavioural traits. The gene products A^1, B^1, C^1, and D^1 may affect many traits, and conversely, traits may be affected by the products of many genes. The boxes show the probable increased environmental component of behavioural traits compared with biochemical and physiological traits.

heredity and environment. These comments also apply to physiological and morphological traits. However, compared with such traits the problem of obtaining an objective measure for behavioural traits may pose far greater difficulties.

The probable reason why the study of the genetic control of behavioural traits has lagged compared with the genetic control of biochemical, physiological, and morphological traits, is because of the need for rather sophisticated experiments to separate clearly genotype from environment, and to assess the importance of interactions between genotype and environment. This is a major reason why definitive work on the genetic control of behaviour has been restricted to a few organisms.

In some animals, notably *Drosophila* and certain laboratory rodents, strains are kept in the laboratory for experimental purposes which have been inbred by brother–sister or sib-mating for many generations. They are, in theory, highly homozygous. The high level or complete homozygosity of certain inbred strains of mice has been clearly shown by the acceptance of grafts between the individuals of a given inbred strain, since presumably the members of a strain are antigenically identical. The same is true for the hybrids between a pair of given inbred strains, since being formed from a cross between two homozygous strains, there will be no segregation in the hybrids. The existence of inbred strains and their hybrids provides a valuable research tool in many fields, in particular behaviour. This is because a large number of genetically identical individuals can be studied for the trait under analysis. The variability of animals within strains and given hybrids will be purely environmental, but because strains and hybrids differ from each other, the variability between strains and hybrids will be genetic as well as environmental. Thus it is possible, by looking at the variability of a trait within and between strains and hybrids, to find out to what extent the trait is controlled by the genotype and by the environment. This approach has been used for behavioural traits in *Drosophila* and laboratory rodents.

Another approach is to take a population of animals and select for extremes over a series of generations for a given trait. If there is a response to selection this usually implies some genetic control of the trait. By analysing the behavioural and genetic nature of the extremes after selection, information on the genetic control of behaviour may emerge. In behavioural research, this approach has been used for traits such as geotaxis and mating speed in species of *Drosophila*, and for certain traits in rodents. As will be seen in Chapter Four, it is potentially a very valuable research method, but has not been exploited greatly in behavioural research.

Turning to man, it is clear that neither of these approaches are possible. Because of the genetic uniqueness of men, except in the case of identical twins, each genotype is represented once only. It is not therefore surprising that comparisons of identical and non-identical twins have assumed so much importance in research on human heredity, for they do enable an assessment of the relative influences of genotype and environment in the determination of a trait, although the common environment of twins, except for those reared apart, leads to difficulties in interpretation. Work on the genetic, and in some cases on the biochemical control of behaviour in man is well developed for single genes with a behavioural effect, simply because medical science does not condone the removal of the unfit, as regularly occurs in other organisms. A severe problem in man for quantitative traits is the question of objective measurement. Many of the traits studied are selected because of their social significance, e.g. intelligence, psychoses, and other psychiatric problems. These are all traits for which objective measurement is almost impossible, and for which single genes are not usually apparent. Thus in man, apart from obvious single gene effects, it is frequently difficult to do more than make vague statements on the possible effects of heredity and environment in the determination of a trait.

When studying the genetic control of behaviour in a series of organisms, it must be remembered that in the phylogenetic series there is an enormous range of complexity of behaviour (Dethier and Stellar, 1964). Early in the phylogenetic series, behaviour is largely a matter of a stimulus triggering a response sequence. Thus the organism is bound by the stimulus and behaviour is stereotyped. This type of behaviour is referred to as *innate*, and is presumably a relatively direct outcome of the properties of the nervous system of the species in question. Later in the phylogenetic series we come to the stage where behaviour is more variable and is modifiable through experience. These adaptations developed by an organism through experience are *acquired*.

Considering the main organisms to be discussed in this book, namely the insect *Drosophila*, laboratory rodents, and man, there are clear differences in the types of behaviour found. Thus innate behaviour is important in *Drosophila*. The important categories are the taxes, which are direct orientations of the whole organism in response to stimuli, the reflexes which are responses of part of the body of the organism to stimuli, and instinctive behaviour, e.g. mating behaviour. So far as acquired behaviour is concerned, it is probably of minor importance in *Drosophila*, although further research may modify our view. In small rodents there is a greater balance between innate and acquired behaviour. Learning, which is a form of acquired behaviour, is important as is shown in experiments on the ability to run mazes, and on conditioned avoidance responses. In man, acquired behaviour such as learning and reasoning reach their greatest development, while innate behaviour is less important.

The variations in the importance of the types of behaviour according to the phylogenetic position of the species has certain implications in behavioural research. For example, the nature of the traits usually studied varies between organisms, e.g. *Drosophila* work has concentrated on traits such as mating behaviour, geotaxis, and phototaxis, which are all essentially innate. This is convenient, as experience is relatively unimportant; so interpretations at the gene level may be easier to make than in rodents, where experience may be more important. In rodents, unless extreme care is taken to standardize experimental conditions, previous experience may be a serious complicating factor, and would make it difficult to make accurate genetic interpretations. In man, as we have already seen, it is extremely difficult to get objective results at all, and now a further problem arises in that experience in the form of learning and reasoning will complicate issues so much that in some instances statements on the genetic control of behaviour may become so vague that they are unconvincing. However, in rodents and man, a promising future field of research is the relationship of genes, biochemical variants, and behaviour, which is now beginning to develop partly because of the detailed biochemical information available for these species.

It is a major aim of this book to discuss how it is possible to obtain reliable and unbiased statements on the relative influence of heredity and environment in the control of behaviour. In some cases it will be shown that it is possible to gain an idea of the genetic architecture of the traits under study. Evolutionary implications of behavioural variations will be discussed, especially in *Drosophila*.

CHAPTER TWO

Single Genes, Inversions, and Behaviour

2.1 *Introduction*

The simplest and easiest type of behavioural variations to investigate are those under the control of a single gene. Many such genes are rare and deleterious and so may not be of great importance in a population, but, because they are discrete entities, the genotypes they control may provide information on the types of behavioural variations which occur in the species in question, and which may possibly be investigated using the biometrical methods to be discussed in the next chapter. The investigation of single genes with behavioural components has been particularly well developed in man, since rare defects are much more likely to survive than in other organisms (see Chapter Seven). In rodents, in particular mice, there are also a number of such genes known (see Chapter Six).

As well as behaviour controlled by rare genes, there are behavioural variants associated with the genotypes making up a polymorphism. A polymorphism occurs when two or more distinct forms of a species occur in an interbreeding population in such frequencies that the rarest of them cannot be maintained by recurrent mutation. The occurrence of a polymorphism indicates a situation of particular genetic and evolutionary interest, as there must be a balance of selective forces maintaining the forms in the population. Thus any behavioural differences associated with polymorphisms are of major evolutionary interest. We shall discuss polymorphisms for the karyotypes of certain species of *Drosophila*, and polymorphisms in certain Lepidoptera in which visual recognition by predators plays a major part. The predators, usually birds, provide a strong selective force, so having major consequences on the genetic constitution of the prey. This last situation is rather distinct from the study of the direct behavioural components of various genotypes, but is included because of its evolutionary significance.

2.2 The mating behaviour of yellow and wild type in Drosophila melanogaster

As an example of variation in behaviour due to a single rare mutant gene, we will discuss in some detail the mating behaviour of the yellow mutant in *Drosophila melanogaster* and compare it with the corresponding wild type. In 1915 Sturtevant noted that yellow males were usually unsuccessful compared with wild males when competing for females. It seemed possible that this was because the behaviour of yellow males differed from wild males, making them less stimulating to the females.

Bastock (1956) studied the detailed mating behaviour of yellow and wild types. The wild stock was crossed to the yellow stock for seven generations, so that the wild stock became genetically similar to the yellow stock except in the region of the yellow locus. All the observations were made on pair matings for flies aged four to five days, the

TABLE 2.1   Percentage success in one hour from pair matings using yellow and wild-type *Drosophila melanogaster*

(After Bastock, 1956)

	Before *crossing the wild stock to the yellow stock for seven generations*	After *crossing the wild stock to the yellow stock for seven generations*
Wild ♂ × wild ♀	62	75
Yellow ♂ × wild ♀	34	47
Wild ♂ × yellow ♀	87	81
Yellow ♂ × yellow ♀	78	59

males and females having been kept in separate vials after emergence for this time. The percentage successes in one hour are given in Table 2.1. The yellow × yellow percentage success is far lower than for wild × wild. In considering matings between yellow and wild type, the yellow male × wild female percentage success is lower than

B

the wild male × yellow female. Thus in the crosses where there are yellow males, the percentage success is much lower than where there are wild-type males. The success of a given female therefore depends on the type of male. Hence the difference in behaviour seems to reside largely in the reduced mating success of the yellow male compared with the wild-type male.

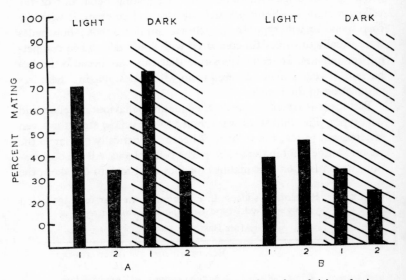

FIG. 2.1 Percentage of matings in one hour for winged (1) and wingless (2) males, and normal (A) and antennaless (B) females, from experiments carried out in the light and the dark in *D. melanogaster*. (After Bastock, 1956.)

Bastock then proceeded to analyse the components of courtship behaviour by splitting it into three components, namely:

(1) *Orientation* – which occurs at the beginning of courtship and involves the approach and the following of the female by the male.

(2) *Vibration* – which is the wing display of the male following orientation. Vibration is repeated at short intervals followed by periods of rest. The wing vibrated is usually the one nearer the head of

the female, who receives the stimulus via her antenna. The importance of the male wing display and its perception by the antenna of the female can be shown by studying the mating success of combinations of winged and wingless males, and females with and without antennae. Fig. 2.1, taken from Bastock (1956), shows that the wingless males are much less successful than the normal males when mating with normal females. If the females are antennaless, the mating success for both types of males is low. The winged males are presumably unable to stimulate the antennaless female as well as normal females. Hence the wings of males and antennae of females are important in courtship. Visual stimuli seem unimportant in the courtship of *D. melanogaster* because there is little difference between experiments carried out in the light or dark (Fig. 2.1).

(3) *Licking* is the final stage of courtship when the male goes behind the female, licks her genitalia with his proboscis, and attempts to copulate.

Bastock noted the activity of the males every $1\frac{1}{2}$ seconds during the first $2\frac{1}{2}$ minutes of the courtship of wild-type and yellow males with wild-type females. The percentage of each courtship (disregarding

TABLE 2.2   Analysis of courtship of wild and yellow males
with wild females in *D. melanogaster*
(After Bastock, 1956)

	No. of records out of 100 in which courtship activities were shown	Courtship records			Bout length*	
		Orientation (O)	Vibration (V)	Licking (L)	Average V + L	O
Wild-type female × wild-type male	92	72	22	6	3·9	5·5
Wild-type female × yellow male	83	77	18	6	2·9	6·9
Probability	0·05	0·05	0·05	Not significant	0·01	Not significant

* Bout length is expressed in units of $1\frac{1}{2}$ seconds.

periods when the male was not courting) that consisted of the three elements, orientation, licking, and vibration, was then assessed (Table 2.2). From this table it can be concluded that the yellow males have a lower vibration percentage than wild-type males. Furthermore, if the average bout length, consisting of vibration +

licking is compared, the yellow male has a significantly shorter bout length than wild-type males. This is a reasonable measure of courtship activity, as licking is momentarily superimposed on vibration during a vibration bout. Thus the yellow male is generally less vigorous than the wild-type male in courtship behaviour. Furthermore, the orientation phase of yellow males is longer than that of wild-type males, showing that they take longer to become motivated. Hence the yellow mutant alters behaviour by generally affecting sexual motivation and the quality of courtship stimulation of the males.

The idea that the behavioural change consists of the female's reaction to changed colour or scent of the males is rejected on several grounds:

(1) There is no difference in the behaviour of the wild female to the two types of males during courtship.

(2) When courting *D. simulans* females, the average bout length is greater in wild-type than in yellow males. Furthermore, *D. simulans* females reject both types of males equally.

(3) The relative success of wild and yellow males in the light and dark is unaltered; similarly, the relative success is unchanged comparing females with and without antennae. If females reacted against the yellow males because of changed scent or appearance, it would be expected that the elimination of these stimuli would reduce the difference in the success of the two types of males.

It is finally desirable to inquire to what extent the behavioural patterns depend on the mutant under investigation, and to what extent they depend on the genetic background. Bastock gave data for the percentage success obtained in one hour before crossing the wild stock with yellow stock for seven generations (Table 2.1), showing a significant difference between females as well as between males, whereas after seven generations of crossing the wild stock to the yellow stock, there was no female effect. The initial high yellow female receptivity is probably partly dependent on the genetic background. It can be argued that the receptivity of yellow females will need to be relatively high in view of the low level of stimulus offered by the yellow males.

Some time has been spent on this work because of its detailed behavioural analysis. As will be seen in Chapter Five, differences in mating success have been reported for many mutant strains in *Drosophila*, perhaps attributable to differences in physiological (and sexual) vigour, although detailed analyses of the type described here have not often been carried out.

2.3 *Polymorphisms and inversions in Drosophila*

In natural populations of *D. pseudoobscura*, *D. persimilis*, and many other species of *Drosophila*, polymorphisms for chromosomal inversion sequences are common. The inversion sequences are effectively single gene complexes, since few recombinants are viable from the heterokaryotypes due to the mechanics of meiosis. A great deal of experimental work in *D. pseudoobscura* has shown the heterokaryotypes to be at a selective advantage over the corresponding homokaryotypes. For example, when two sequences Standard (ST) and Chiricahua (CH) were introduced into population cages, which are containers in which a reasonably large population can be maintained over a number of generations, it was found that the ultimate frequencies were about $\frac{2}{3}$ ST and $\frac{1}{3}$ CH, irrespective of the initial inversion frequencies (Wright and Dobzhansky, 1946). Thus the populations reached an equilibrium point for the inversion frequencies. The simplest explanation of such an equilibrium under the relatively constant environment of the population cage is that the heterokaryotypes are at a selective advantage over the homokaryotypes, since this can be shown theoretically to be a condition for a stable equilibrium (Fisher, 1922, and see below). Other pairs of inversions also gave characteristic equilibria. The F_2 between ST and CH and some other pairs of polymorphic inversions show an excess of heterokaryotypes (Dobzhansky, 1947 *a*) due to the selective elimination of homokaryotypic larvae under high levels of competition. More recent experiments have shown the general superiority of polymorphic populations compared with monomorphic populations for traits such as biomass (Beardmore, Dobzhansky, and Pavlovsky, 1960) and capacity for increase (Dobzhansky, Lewontin, and Pavlovsky, 1964).

In natural populations some of the inversion sequences show cyclical temporal changes in frequencies (Dobzhansky, 1947 *b*) on an annual basis, and there are regular changes with altitude (Dobzhansky, 1948). Part of the explanation may lie in the differential adaptation of the inversion sequences to regular annual changes in factors such as temperature and competition (Birch, 1955). Certainly the results of population cage experiments are very temperature dependent, the equilibria cited above being obtained at 25° C, but different results are found at lower temperatures. The regular annual and altitudinal changes in inversion sequences are then not unexpected, and constitute a method of accommodating regular environmental variations and other types of environmental heterogeneity, by giving populations greater powers to adapt to a multiplicity of environments.

In other *Drosophila* species where polymorphic inversion systems are known, the fitness factors associated with specific inversions have been examined less completely than in *D. pseudoobscura*, but such evidence as has emerged shows the general superiority of the heterokaryotypes. Because of the fitness factors found to be associated with karyotypic combinations, it is reasonable to inquire into the possibility of the association of behavioural traits with karyotypes. Before reviewing the evidence it is desirable to show that a stable equilibrium is expected when the heterozygote at a locus is fitter than both homozygotes. From the point of view of the derivation, the ST and CH inversions can be formally regarded as two alleles at a locus.

Let the two alleles at a locus A and a, have gene frequencies p and q respectively, such that $p + q = 1$. Under random mating the gene frequencies will be fixed from generation to generation except for random variation. The simplest way of showing this is to follow what happens under random union of gametes, which in many (but not all) situations is implied by random mating. Thus there will be a proportion p of A genes and q of a genes, so the gametes in each sex can be formally expressed as:

$$pA + qa.$$

If these unite at random the genotypic proportions in the next generation will be given by

$$(pA + qa)^2 = p^2AA + 2pqAa + q^2aa.$$

The gene frequency of A in this generation is given by the frequency of AA plus half of the frequency of Aa $= p^2 + pq = p(p + q) = p$, and similarly the gene frequency of gene $a = q$. This is the Hardy–Weinberg Law, so named after its two discoverers. This result is only strictly true in infinitely large populations, since in finite populations p and q will vary somewhat, due to random variation.

We must now introduce the complication of different fitnesses for each genotype. Let the fitnesses of the genotypes AA, Aa, and aa be $1 - s_1$, 1, and $1 - s_2$. Then the genotypic proportions before and after selection can be written:

Genotypes	AA	Aa	aa	Tota
Fitnesses	$1 - s_1$	1	$1 - s_2$	
Frequencies before selection	p^2	$2pq$	q^2	1
Frequencies after selection	$p^2(1 - s_1)$	$2pq$	$q^2(1 - s_2)$	W

If p^1 and q^1 represent the gene frequencies in the next generation then

$$p^1 = \frac{p^2 - p^2 s_1 + pq}{W} = \frac{p - s_1 p^2}{W}$$

and

$$q^1 = \frac{pq + q^2 - q^2 s_2}{W} = \frac{q - s_2 q^2}{W}.$$

It is necessary to divide by W so that $p^1 + q^1 = p + q = 1$. We wish to find out what ultimately happens to this population. One question is whether at any stage gene frequencies remain unchanged from generation to generation at an equilibrium, apart from random variations. If the change in gene frequency is written as Δp, then it will be expected that $\Delta p = p^1 - p = 0$ at an equilibrium. Substituting the value of p^1 given above into this equation yields three solutions. Two are trivial, namely $p = 0$ and 1 when either the population will be all AA or aa, which does not correspond to a polymorphic situation. A third solution is $p_e = \dfrac{s_2}{s_1 + s_2}$ so that $q_e = \dfrac{s_1}{s_1 + s_2}$ because $p_e + q_e = 1$. The values p_e and q_e are called the equilibrium gene frequencies since they are unchanged in an infinite population. It will be noted that p_e and q_e depend only on the selective values

s_1 and s_2, so that irrespective of the initial values of p and q, the same equilibrium is expected. Now for p_e and q_e to exist, either $s_1, s_2 > 0$ or $s_1, s_2 < 0$, since if s_1 and s_2 are of dissimilar sign, either p_e or q_e will be < 0 which is impossible. It can be shown that the equilibrium is stable if $s_1, s_2 > 0$, that is A$a >$ AA, aa in fitness. This means that if there is a small displacement from p_e, as may occur by chance in a finite population, the population will tend to return to p_e in subsequent generations. Conversely, if $s_1, s_2 < 0$, that is A$a <$ AA, aa in fitness the equilibrium is unstable, since if there is a small displacement from p_e this will be accentuated generation by generation, and ultimately the population will become all AA or aa. Thus, in conclusion, a stable equilibrium is expected if a heterozygote is fitter than its corresponding homozygotes under random mating. In passing we note that when s_1, s_2 are of dissimilar sign, a trivial equilibrium of $p = 1$ will be obtained if $s_1 < 0$ and of $q = 1$ if $s_2 < 0$. This is self-evident since in the former case the fitness relationships are AA $>$ A$a > aa$, and in the latter case $aa >$ A$a >$ AA.

Returning to the inversions of *D. pseudoobscura*, fitnesses of ST/ST, ST/CH, and CH/CH of 0·7, 1, and 0·4 respectively corresponding to $s_1 = 0·3$ and $s_2 = 0·6$ are realistic. These give $p_e = 0·67$ and $q_e = 0·33$ corresponding approximately to the frequencies obtained in the population cages at equilibrium. Thus heterokaryotype advantage provides a reasonable explanation of the results in the population cages.

However, it must be pointed out that the occurrence of a polymorphism does not always depend on the fitness of the heterozygote being fitter than the homozygotes. A polymorphism is basically a method of maintaining genetic variability in an outbred population, and any method of maintaining such variability, whether it be environmental heterogeneity, mating behaviour variations, non-random fertilization, or density-dependent fitnesses of genotypes, may still in theory lead to a polymorphism. There are many theoretical papers discussing the consequences of all these and other systems.

2.4 *Inversion sequences and mating behaviour in Drosophila*

In *D. pseudoobscura* Spiess and Langer (1964 *a*) have shown substantial mating speed differences between homokaryotypes derived from stocks collected at Mather, California. They used homokaryotypes for the ST, CH, TL (Tree Line), PP (Pikes Peak), and AR (Arrow-

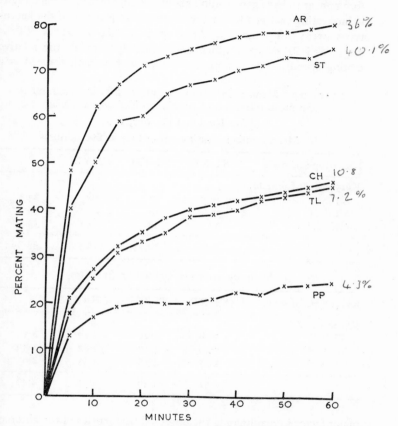

FIG. 2.2 Cumulative percentage curves for homokaryotype homogamic matings over a one-hour period (based on 300 pairs per curve) in *D. pseudoobscura.* AR = Arrowhead, ST = Standard, CH = Chiricahua, TL = Tree Line, PP = Pikes Peak. (After Spiess and Langer, 1964 *a*.)

head) inversions. Mating was carried out at 25° C for flies six days old, using ten pairs per mating chamber. In Fig. 2.2 are the cumulative percentage curves for homokaryotypic homogamic matings over a one-hour period. The only contrasts not significant at sixty minutes are AR versus ST, and CH versus TL. The homokaryotypes therefore appear to have gene complexes controlling mating behaviour. It is interesting that at Mather the observed frequencies of the karyotypes were ST = 40·1%, AR = 36·0%, CH = 10·8%, TL = 7·2%, and PP = 4·3% which approximately parallels the relative mating speeds. It is tempting to suppose that mating speed is a

TABLE 2.3   Mean numbers mating out of fifty in five minutes and mean durations of copulation in *D. pseudoobscura*

(After Kaul and Parsons, 1965)

(a) Mean numbers mating out of fifty in five minutes

Karyotype of male	ST/ST	ST/CH	CH/CH	$\bar{x}$
Karyotype of female:				
ST/ST	39·5	37·5	26·5	34·5
ST/CH	36	40	23·5	33·17
CH/CH	37	33	26·5	32·17
	37·5	36·83	25·5	33·28

(b) Mean durations of copulation (minutes)

Karyotype of male	ST/ST	ST/CH	CH/CH	
Karotype of female				
ST/ST	5·08	4·22	3·17	4·16
ST/CH	5·49	4·47	3·82	4·59
CH/CH	5·95	4·38	3·55	4·63
	5·51	4·36	3·51	4·46

major factor in maintaining the observed frequencies of the chromosomes in this population (Spiess and Langer, 1964 a). Whether or not this is true, it is clear that differences in mating speeds may be important in controlling the frequencies of the chromosomes in natural populations.

On the grounds that the heterokaryotypes contribute as much or more to future generations as the homokaryotypes, Kaul and Parsons (1965) studied both the average mating speed and the duration of copulation of all possible combinations between the three karyotypic combinations ST/ST, ST/CH, and CH/CH using vials with single pairs of flies, so making it possible easily to assess the duration of copulation. In Table 2.3 the mean numbers mating out of fifty in five minutes are given. Inspection of the marginal frequencies shows that males of the ST/ST and ST/CH karyotypes have similar mating frequencies, and males of CH/CH karyotype have a lower mating frequency. There is little difference between karyotypes for females, thus mating frequencies are almost entirely male determined. From Table 2.3 it is also clear that duration of copulation is mainly male determined, with the shortest durations for CH/CH males, followed by ST/CH and ST/ST. There is thus a negative correlation between mating frequency and duration of copulation for different karyotypes in the males. Hence the sum of the mean mating speed and duration of copulation is more equal than the component times (Table 2.4),

TABLE 2.4 Comparison of mean mating speeds and durations of copulation (minutes) in *D. pseudoobscura*
(After Kaul and Parsons, 1965)

Karyo-type	Females			Males		
	Mating speed	Duration of copulation	Sum	Mating speed	Duration of copulation	Sum
ST/ST	2·33	4·16	6·49	2·03	5·51	7·54
ST/CH	2·69	4·59	7·28	2·15	4·36	6·51
CH/CH	2·65	4·63	7·28	4·76	3·51	8·27

so that mating speed and duration of copulation may possibly be regarded as an integrated system controlled mainly by the male. The sum of the components is less for the heterokaryotypes than the homokaryotypes in males, and therefore represents an example of heterokaryotype advantage restricted to males. It may be of some selective advantage to complete mating and copulation rapidly, since those individuals finishing most rapidly may most readily leave genes in subsequent generations.

Even more recently, Spiess, Langer, and Spiess (1966) have studied mating speeds for a number of combinations using the technique of ten pairs of flies per mating chamber as described above (Fig. 2.2), and found that male heterokaryotypes consistently had a faster mating speed than the corresponding homokaryotypes. Durations of copulation were not, however, studied. Far more work needs to be done on the behavioural consequences of different karyotypes in *D. pseudoobscura*, studying, for example, the effects of different genetic backgrounds, collection sites, and environments such as variations in temperature, age, and lighting.

The importance of temperature as an environmental variable is clearly shown in a discussion of some data of Parsons and Kaul (1966 *a*) in the next chapter for the AR/AR, AR/PP, and PP/PP karyotypes. Spiess, Langer, and Spiess (1966) have shown temperature and age effects for AR/AR and PP/PP homokaryotypes. Parsons and Kaul (1966 *a*) found relatively small differences in mating speeds between AR/AR and PP/PP homokaryotypes compared with Spiess and Langer (1964 *a*) who found substantial differences. Although environmental variables are no doubt a partial explanation, evidence of Spiess, Langer, and Spiess (1966) suggests that there are substantial differences between strains of given karyotypes, even though all strains were collected from the same locality, Mather. Parsons and Kaul (1967) give similar evidence for strains of ST/ST and CH/CH homokaryotypes, also collected at Mather. Thus, according to the strains used in the experiments, rather different results may be obtained for a given karyotype because of differing genetic backgrounds.

Until one can assess the nature and magnitude of all these various complicating factors, we cannot generalize readily from specific experiments to the general control of behaviour by inversion systems.

A recent observation by Ehrman *et al.* (1965) is of particular significance. Using homokaryotypic strains of AR and CH, some of which had been selected for geotaxis, they observed mating behaviour in an observation chamber (see Fig. 5.1) with twenty to twenty-five pairs of flies made up of equal proportions of AR to CH in certain experiments, and unequal proportions in others. In many cases the minority genotypes were more successful in mating than when they were in the majority. The physiological basis of this phenomenon is unknown, but mating advantages correlated with genotype frequencies may have considerable implications. Thus if two or more karyotypes are each more successful in mating when they are rare than when they are frequent, the fitness of these karyotypes will grow as their frequencies diminish, and fall as their frequencies increase. In theory this could lead to a balanced polymorphism in the absence of heterozygote advantage. If common in natural populations, this phenomenon would be of some significance in evolution, since it provides yet another way of increasing genetic variability.

Spiess and Langer (1964 b) studied mating speeds in D. persimilis for the Whitney (WT) and Klamath (KL) inversions. Direct observation was carried out on groups of ten flies of each sex at 20° C for flies aged eight days. One set of results is given in Fig. 2.3. As well as homogamic matings between the WT/WT and KL/KL homokaryotypes, the two possible heterogamic matings were carried out. Both crosses with WT/WT females show greater mating speeds than crosses with KL/KL females, thus the WT/WT females mate rapidly and the KL/KL females mate slowly irrespective of the male karyotype. Hence, in contrast with the D. pseudoobscura results, the karyotype of the female is important in determining mating speed. However, for a given female karyotype, WT/WT males have a somewhat faster mating speed than KL/KL males. Although the difference is relatively small compared with the difference between karyotypes of females, it does show that the karyotype of the male as well as the karyotype of the female plays a part in determining mating speed.

Observations on actual mating behaviour have shown that WT/WT females accept males readily, while KL/KL females tend to refuse males, and that WT/WT males court more actively than do KL/KL males. The differences for the various combinations can therefore be interpreted in terms of the relative intensities of the copulation tendency of males and the avoidance tendency of females. Earlier experiments (Spiess and Langer 1961) demonstrated for matings over a twenty-four-hour period, that male mating propensity was the

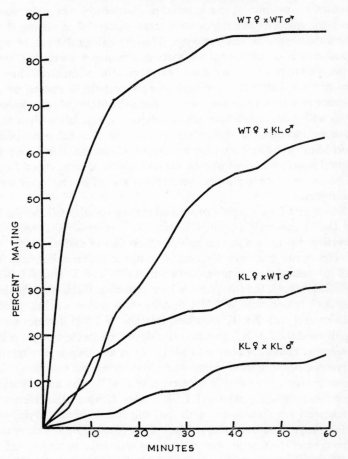

FIG. 2.3 Cumulative percentage curves for homokaryotype matings over a one-hour period in *D. persimilis* (based on 60 pairs per curve). KL = Klamath, WT = Whitney. (After Spiess and Langer, 1964 *b*.)

important feature as WT/WT males mated significantly more than KL/KL males, with no large differences according to the karyotype of the females. Thus, depending on the time after commencing the experiment, somewhat different results may occur, which are interpretable in terms of factors such as the relative intensities of copulation and avoidance tendencies, and the likelihood of multiple matings for a given individual which probably occurs more for males than for females. This temporal factor will be further discussed in the next chapter.

Spiess and Langer (1964 b) also carried out some experiments using heterokaryotypes WT/KL, and found them to have a mating speed intermediate between the homokaryotypes for homogamic matings, although if the heterokaryotypes were mated to homokaryotypes, the mating speed was fast or slow according to the mating speed of the homokaryotype.

The results described are for flies derived from White Woolf, California. Spiess and Langer studied mating speeds for homogamic matings between the two homokaryotypes from Mather, California, and found that WT/WT homogamic matings occurred somewhat faster than KL/KL homogamic matings in agreement with the above results, but the difference was far less marked than at White Woolf. This provides evidence for some differences between localities, without, however, disturbing the overall picture, but clearly a great deal of further research is necessary.

There is a large field for investigation in view of the number of polymorphic inversion systems that have been described in various species of *Drosophila*. Among other species perhaps *D. pavani*, a species living in central Chile and on the eastern slopes of the Andes in Argentina, has been looked at in most detail. In most natural populations the heterokaryotypes exist in fairly uniform frequencies. Mating ability of the males was assessed by using virgin females of a sibling species *D. gaucha* having a standard gene arrangement. It was found that males heterozygous for the gene arrangements under study were superior in mating activity to the corresponding homokaryotypes within the same population (Brncic and Koref-Santibañez, 1964). It is argued, therefore, that the superiority in mating activity of the heterokaryotypes may be an important factor in the maintenance of balanced polymorphisms in natural populations.

The results discussed in this section thus clearly show that inversion karyotypes are associated with differences in mating behaviour. An extremely difficult problem is that of how we are to argue from laboratory experiments carried out under controlled conditions to the wild. However, laboratory experiments will at least give clues as to the types of behavioural phenomena to be studied in the wild, and the extent to which traits vary with the environment.

2.5 Industrial melanism and mimicry

There is much evidence to show that predators hunt by sight and destroy their prey selectively, so killing a greater proportion of those individuals that do not fit into their background well. Many examples of this type of situation have been described (see, for example, Ford, 1964). In this section we will briefly mention two such situations in the Lepidoptera where predators (characteristically various species of birds) recognize individuals by their colour and pattern and may therefore take them, unless by some means the prey can become protected.

Since the middle of the last century, many species of moths inhabiting certain highly industrialized regions have been becoming decidedly darker. These moths often rest fully exposed on tree trunks and rocks, and are protected from predators by having a cryptic resemblance to their background. Since industrialisation the background has become much darker, so the original light-coloured moths would become much more visible to predators. For this reason, presumably, many species have evolved darker melanic forms, often controlled by a single gene locus. The classic case is that of *Biston betularia* studied extensively by Kettlewell (1956), in which dark forms began to appear in the middle of the last century in the industrial regions of Great Britain. The dark form, termed *carbonaria*, is controlled by a dominant gene. Kettlewell (1956; see also Ford, 1964) carried out a series of classic experiments in the field demonstrating differential predation in rural unpolluted and industrial polluted regions, such that in the rural regions the *betularia* form was favoured, and in the industrial regions the *carbonaria* form. Thus differential predation can lead to rapid genetic changes in the prey.

The second situation to be discussed is that of mimicry, which is rather more complex. There are two types of mimicry:

Müllerian mimicry. If there are two species which are distasteful to a predator living in the same locality, and their mutual predators learn to avoid them by their appearance, then fewer will be killed by predators if they have similar appearances than if they have different appearances, since this represents a less complex learning situation for the predator. Thus there will be selection for increased resemblance between them and against polymorphism.

Batesian mimicry. If there is a species which is warningly coloured and distasteful to a predator, then an edible species may gain protection from a common predator if it resembles the warningly coloured species sufficiently closely to be mistaken for it. The edible species is referred to as the *mimic* and the inedible warningly coloured species the *model*. This type of mimicry tends to produce a polymorphism within the edible species consisting of the mimic and a non-mimetic form, because the advantage to the mimic wanes as it becomes commoner, since the higher the proportion of mimics the less frequently will the predator take the inedible model.

In spite of the apparent theoretical distinction between Müllerian and Batesian mimicry, it may in practice be extremely difficult to distinguish between the two (Fisher, 1930). For example, a species may be a Müllerian mimic of another so far as one species of predator is concerned, and a Batesian mimic from the point of view of another predator (Sheppard, 1963).

In butterflies in which Batesian mimicry has been investigated genetically, the difference between mimetic and non-mimetic forms in a given edible species is nearly always determined by a single switch gene, dominant in effect. The frequent good resemblance of the mimic to the model probably began as a mutant having a poor resemblance, followed by a readjustment of the genotype by natural selection to improve the effect of the major gene towards more perfect mimicry. Clarke and Sheppard (see Sheppard, 1963, and Ford, 1964, for references) in a series of breeding experiments have shown this interpretation to be essentially correct in the highly polymorphic butterfly *Papilio dardanus*. That the perfection of mimicry has evolved is clear, since when the major genes controlling the polymorphism are put into the gene complexes of different races, the mimicry becomes less perfect. Furthermore, during the evolution of perfect mimicry, dominance evolves so that the heterozygote appears like one of the homozygotes (the mimetic one). Evidence for this

C

comes from the common breakdown of dominance in hybrids between races.

Without going into further details, it should be clear that for Batesian mimicry, predation by one species based on visual recognition, can lead to complex genetic changes in the prey. The system is essentially based on the fact that if a predator takes an inedible form, it will, for a period, tend to avoid that form, so a certain proportion of mimics of that form can gain protection. The degree of distastefulness may well be relevant; a very distasteful model protecting more mimics than a less distasteful one. Duncan and Sheppard (1965) have presented indirect evidence for this from an experiment they carried out in the laboratory, where Batesian mimicry was simulated by using chickens as predators and green-coloured drinking solutions of various strengths as their prey. The darkest solution represented a model and when taken a shock was administered to the bird. Two levels of shock were used, and the resultant behaviour of the birds depended on the level of shock to which they had become accustomed, such that at the higher level the birds tended to avoid more completely the solutions with colours near that giving the shock, than at the lower level. It is argued from this result, that if the penalty accruing to a predator is severe, then mimicry will not need to be as perfect as when the penalty is mild, since a severe penalty will lead to a much stronger degree of avoidance than a mild penalty. More mimics will probably be protected if the predator receives a severe penalty compared with a mild penalty.

Thus genetic changes may occur in certain species as a result of a tendency to protect themselves against predation. This is no doubt a general tendency. Another group of organisms where predation by birds is important are the land snails which have various colour and banding forms on their shells controlled by polymorphic loci. The level of predation of a given form depends on the background environment which determines whether the snail is concealed from the predator or not. Cain and Sheppard (1954) have carried out a great deal of work, showing the great range of phenotype frequencies according to background environment in *Cepaea nemoralis*. Further work in this and related species is summarized by Ford (1964).

2.6. *Conclusions*

The rather limited results presented show that large differences in behaviour may be associated with single genes and inversions. From the population point of view the polymorphic inversion systems of *Drosophila* are of particular importance, even though we are far from knowing what actually happens in natural populations. This is one difficulty inherent in all laboratory studies, but they will help us decide on the types of behaviour that can be studied in nature. From this point of view, there is clearly a great need to find out how the genetic background and environment will modify behaviour controlled by major genes and inversions, and in the next chapter methods are discussed with this aim.

In the case of industrial melanism and mimicry, where polymorphisms for colour and pattern forms occur as a consequence of visual recognition leading to differential predation, we have the direct modification of the genotype of the prey in response to the predator. These are polymorphisms controlled essentially by an intimate and definable interaction between two or more species. We are not studying the behaviour of the forms making up the polymorphism, but merely their potential for being preyed on, and genetic modifications consequent upon this. However, it is much easier to see the evolutionary implications of variations in predations rates, than of the various modifications of mating behaviour in *Drosophila* which have hardly been related to the situation in nature.

CHAPTER THREE

Quantitative Traits

3.1 *The nature of continuous variation*

Much of the variation discussed in the previous chapter is under the control of specific loci or inversions that can be assigned to positions on chromosomes. However, most behavioural traits are quantitative rather than qualitative. This means that it is not possible to split the population under study into discrete groups for the trait. Variation of this type, without natural discontinuities, is referred to as continuous variation.

The nature of continuous variation can be most easily looked at by considering a graph of the heights of men in classes with one-inch intervals plotted against the percentages of the population in each of these classes (Fig. 3.1). This is therefore a *discrete frequency distribution* of heights. If the number of classes is made progressively smaller, and the number of individuals measured is progressively increased, then ultimately a smooth curve would be obtained as in Fig. 3.1. This is therefore a *continuous frequency distribution* of heights. The frequency distributions of many quantitative traits approximate more or less closely to the *normal distribution*. The normal distribution has been studied mathematically and can be completely described in terms of two quantities or *parameters*. One is the mean or average value. If x_i is an individual observation and there are n observations, then the mean $\bar{x}$ is given by

$$\bar{x} = \frac{\sum x_i}{n} \tag{3.1}$$

The other quantity is an expression of variability around the mean. In some cases the variability around the mean will be small, and in

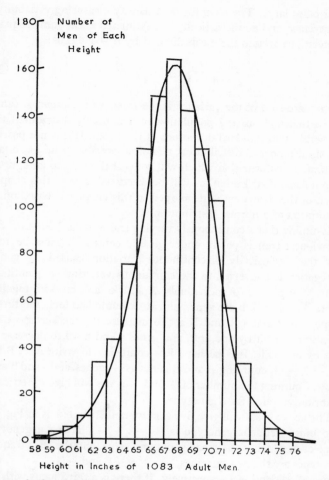

FIG. 3.1 A frequency distribution of heights of 1,083 adult men. The blocks indicate the actual number of men whose heights were within the unit range of one inch. The smooth curve is a normal curve based on the mean and standard deviation of the data. (After Villee, 1964.)

other cases large. The term for the quantity measuring variability is the *variance*, and mathematically it is estimated as the sum of squares of deviations around the mean divided by n — 1 $\bar{x}$ thus:

$$\frac{1}{n-1} \sum (x_i - \bar{x})^2. \qquad (3.2)$$

The square root of the variance is the *standard deviation*. It can be shown that 95% of the population of a normally distributed trait lies within two standard deviations of the mean. If it is not possible to assume a normal distribution, it is often possible to find a suitable algebraic transformation which will convert the data to an approximate normal distribution, as will be discussed later in this chapter. Much of the theory to be developed in this chapter is based on the assumption of a normal distribution.

Assuming that a continuously varying trait such as height or some behavioural trait is partly under genetic control, it must be asked how the intrinsically discontinuous variation caused by genetic segregation is converted to the continuous variation of quantitative traits. Suppose two individuals A/a . B/b are crossed together, where A, a and B, b are gene pairs at two unlinked loci, and further suppose that genes A and B act to increase the measurement of a quantitative trait by one unit, and genes a and b act to decrease the trait by one unit. It is perhaps less confusing to write A/a . B/b as $+/-$. $+/-$, counting A and B genes as $+$ genes, and a and b as $-$ genes. Counting the number of $+$ and $-$ genes will give a metrical or quantitative value for a genotype.

The above cross will give five genotypes distributed as in Fig. 3.2. The most frequent genotype is $+/-$. $+/-$, having a genotypic value of 0, which is the mean genotypic value, and the least frequent genotypes are the two extremes, $+/+$. $+/+$ and $-/-$. $-/-$, with values of $+4$ and -4 respectively. If there is a third locus with two similar alleles affecting height, then for a cross between multiple heterozygotes the number of genotypic classes rises to seven, and with a fourth to nine, and so on. The differences between the classes become progressively smaller as the number of segregating loci rises.

At the stage when the differences between classes become about as small as the error of measurement, the distribution will become continuous. In addition, any variation due to non-genetic causes will blur the underlying discontinuity implied by segregation, so that the variation seen may become continuous irrespective of the accuracy of measurement.

Thus an assumption of many genes, each with small effects, superimposed upon variability due to non-genetic or environmental causes, will lead to a continuous distribution similar to that given in Fig. 3.1. Genes which contribute to a quantitative trait, but which

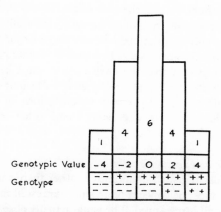

FIG. 3.2 Frequencies of genotypes from the cross $+/-$. $+/-$ × $+/-$. $+/-$ plotted according to the genotypic value (i.e. the relative number of $+$ and $-$ genes). The frequencies of each genotype are given in the histogram.

are not directly identifiable by classical Mendelian segregation (i.e. cannot be studied individually) are referred to as *polygenes*, and genes whose effects can be studied individually are referred to as *major genes*. These categories do not imply any fundamental distinction between the two categories of genes. They are merely a matter of convenience, since the breeding methods used to study the effects of major genes cannot, in general, be used in the study of polygenes. Even so, as will be seen in the next chapter, it is possible under certain circumstances to magnify the effects of polygenes by statistical and perhaps biochemical techniques to such an extent, that to all intents and purposes they behave as major genes.

The synthesis between the study of genes with discrete qualitative effects, and of those controlling continuously varying traits had its origins in a classic paper by Fisher (1918) and was further advanced by Wright (1921), Mather (1949), Kempthorne (1957), Falconer (1960), and others. A branch of genetics called *quantitative* or *biometrical* genetics has grown up to deal with the study of continuous variation.

Behavioural traits, such as the time mice take to run a maze or the duration of copulation in *Drosophila*, are essentially quantitative, thus for their analysis an appreciation of the methods and aims of biometrical genetics is necessary. It should be pointed out here, as it will be at later stages, that the environment must be rigidly controlled for accurate results. This is because behaviour can occasionally be radically altered by minor modifications of temperature, humidity, light, previous experience, and other environmental factors.

3.2 *Phenotypic and genotypic values*

Since we are dealing with quantitative rather than qualitative traits we must introduce the concept of a value, expressed in metric units, by which the trait is measured. The value actually observed when the trait is measured on the individual is its phenotypic value, and all calculations of means and variances must be based on phenotypic values. The aim of biometrical genetics is to divide the phenotypic value into component parts attributable to different causes.

Clearly the first division is into genotypic and environmental components. The genotype is the sum of the particular genes possessed by an individual, and the environment is the sum of all the non-genetic disturbances influencing the phenotypic value. Symbolically we write for an individual (after Falconer, 1960)

$$P = G + E, \tag{3.3}$$

where P is the phenotypic value, G the genotypic value, and E the environmental deviation. The term environmental deviation is used since we can think of the genotype conferring a certain value on an individual, and the environment causing a deviation from this in one direction or another. Arbitrarily we take the mean environmental deviation of the population as a whole to be zero, so the mean phenotypic value (that is, the population mean) is equal to the mean genotypic value.

Since continuously varying traits are being considered we will need the phenotypic variance V_P. From (3.3),

$$V_P = V_G + V_E \qquad (3.4)$$

where V_G and V_E represent the genotypic and environmental variances. This relationship assumes that the genotype and environment are uncorrelated. If this is not the situation, the genotypic variance would be over-estimated if there is a positive correlation between genotype and environment, and under-estimated if there is a negative correlation between genotype and environment. Correlations between genotype and environment can frequently be avoided in the laboratory, but may be important for behavioural traits, in which case we would need to estimate the degree of correlation. We would then need to rewrite the above equation as

$$V_P = V_G + V_E + 2 \ \text{Cov}_{G,E}, \qquad (3.5)$$

where $\text{Cov}_{G,E}$* represents the covariance of genotypic values and environmental deviations, and provides, according to its magnitude, an estimate of the correlation between genotype and environment, or the genotype $\times$ environment interaction. It is one of the aims of biometrical genetics to develop methods for estimating V_G, V_E, and $\text{Cov}_{G,E}$. The remainder of this chapter will be devoted to a discussion of such methods, with particular reference to those that can be used in the study of behavioural traits.

3.3 *Variability of quantitative traits within and between inbred strains*

Inbred strains maintained by brother–sister (sib) mating have been developed in many species, in particular rodents and *Drosophila*.

---

* A detailed discussion of the meaning of covariance is given in most elementary statistics textbooks.

Sib-mating, being a form of inbreeding, leads to a progressive increase of homozygosity in each generation. In fact, the proportion of heterozygotes is expected to fall by a fraction of 19·1% per generation. In theory, such strains will ultimately be completely homozygous. In some cases the approach to homozygosity may be retarded by the heterozygotes being fitter than the corresponding homozygotes. However, assuming that complete homozygosity is attained, then all individuals *within* an inbred strain will be genetically identical, and such variation as does occur will be basically environmental. Between strains there may be variation due to the different genetic constitutions of the strains as well as variation due to the environment. Even if several inbred strains are set up from the same population, the genetic constitutions of the strains will be expected to differ, since by chance different loci are likely to be made homozygous in the different strains.

TABLE 3.1   Duration of copulation in *D. melanogaster*
(After MacBean and Parsons, 1965)
Mean durations of copulation (minutes)
based on fifty-two observations for each strain

Strain	N1	N2	D5	G5	Y2
Mean (minutes)	19·27	16·69	21·42	19·50	17·65

		Analysis of variance			
	d.f.	M.S.		F	E.M.S.
Between strains	4	172·75	M_1	12·34*	$V_E + 52V_G$
Within strains	255	14·00	M_2		V_E

$$* P < 0.001$$
$$V_E = 14.00$$
$$V_G = 3.05$$
$$h^2{}_B = 0.18$$

In Table 3.1 data on the duration of copulation in minutes are given for five inbred strains of *Drosophila melanogaster* which had been sib-mated in the laboratory for at least 140 generations (MacBean and Parsons, 1966). In theory, they should be almost completely homozygous after this period of time. The experimental procedure consisted of separating flies at eclosion, ageing them separately until they were three days of age and then setting up single pair matings. The time until mating commences is the mating speed which was discussed in Section 2.4, and will be discussed further at a later stage in this chapter. Immediately mating commenced, recording of the duration of copulation began (see also Section 2.4). Some variations in mean durations of copulation are apparent as shown by the means in Table 3.1.

To find out if the genotypes of the strains are important in determining the duration of copulation, an analysis of variance must be carried out to ascertain the relative importance of variation within and between strains (Table 3.1). The mean square (variance) within strains is represented by the error component in an analysis of variance. The mean square (variance) between strains is much greater than that within strains, and in fact the variance ratio of $\frac{\text{M.S. between strains}}{\text{M.S. within strains}} = \frac{M_1}{M_2} = 12 \cdot 34$. By consulting tables of the F distribution which can be found in many statistics textbooks, this ratio can be shown to be significant at the $0 \cdot 1\%$ level. Thus the variation between strains is significantly greater than that within strains.

We must now interpret this result genetically. The within strains M.S. represents the variation remaining after taking into account the strains, and is therefore the environmental variance V_E. Thus

$$V_E = M_2 \qquad (3.6)$$

Between strains there are both genotypic and environmental variance components. The expected mean square (E.M.S.) between strains can be shown to be:

$$V_E + rV_G = M_1, \qquad (3.7)$$

where r is the number of replicates for each strain, in this example being fifty-two. Thus by equating the observed mean squares M_1 and M_2 with the expected mean squares we obtain estimates:

$$V_G = \frac{M_1 - M_2}{r} \text{ and } V_E = M_2. \qquad (3.8)$$

The data give $V_G = 3 \cdot 05$ and $V_E = 14 \cdot 00$.

Now the total variance in the population, or phenotypic variance V_P, is equal to $V_G + V_E$, assuming no interaction between genotype and environment (equation 3.4). It is then reasonable to compute the proportion of the phenotypic variance that is genotypic thus

$$\frac{V_G}{V_G + V_E}, \qquad (3.9)$$

which is referred to as the '*heritability in the broad sense*' $h^2{}_B$. In our example $h^2{}_B = 0.18$. Clearly $0 \leq h^2{}_B \leq 1$, for if $h^2{}_B = 0$, then $V_G = 0$, and the trait would be determined entirely by the environment, and if $h^2{}_B = 1$, then $V_E = 0$, so the trait would be determined entirely by the genotype. The figure of 0.18 is not particularly high but it does indicate a degree of genotypic control of the duration of copulation.

It must be stressed that a heritability so estimated is a characteristic of the actual inbred strains under the environmental conditions prevailing. If the experiment were run under different conditions, or with different strains or both, different values may be obtained. If we wish to make inferences about the components of variance and the heritability of a trait in a given population of an outbred species, we must set up inbred strains at random from the population. Then, in theory, the estimates obtained will relate to the parameters of the parent population, rather than to the strains in the sample. This condition may not often be directly fulfilled, but to all intents and purposes, any set of inbred strains will permit more or less realistic estimates to be made. However, in all cases the environment must be accurately defined.

The procedure described may be extended to the study of a behavioural trait in a set of inbred strains over a series of environments. Let us imagine a hypothetical situation where we are studying a behavioural trait which may or may not be associated with mating behaviour. In the experiment there are a inbred strains at b temperatures and c light intensities. Now each strain occurs once in each of r replicates at each temperature and light intensity. The appropriate partition of variance is given in Table 3.2 with degrees of freedom, observed and expected mean squares for the main effects (strains, temperatures, and light intensities), and the interactions between them.

TABLE 3.2 Scheme of analysis of variance for separating out genotypic and various environmental effects

	d.f.	M.S.	E.M.S.
Strains	$a-1$	M_1	$V_E + rV_{abc} + rcV_{ab} + rbV_{ac} + rbcV_a$
Temperatures	$b-1$	M_2	$V_E + rV_{abc} + rcV_{ab} + raV_{bc} + racV_b$
Light intensities	$c-1$	M_3	$V_E + rV_{abc} + rbV_{ac} + raV_{bc} + rabV_c$
Strains × temperatures	$(a-1)(b-1)$	M_4	$V_E + rV_{abc} + rcV_{ab}$
Strains × light intensities	$(a-1)(c-1)$	M_5	$V_E + rV_{abc} + rbV_{ac}$
Temperatures × light intensities	$(b-1)(c-1)$	M_6	$V_E + rV_{abc} + raV_{bc}$
Strains × temperatures × light intensities	$(a-1)(b-1)(c-1)$	M_7	$V_E + rV_{abc}$
Error		M_8	V_E
Total	$abcr - 1$		

$$V_E = M_8$$

$$V_{abc} = \frac{M_7 - M_8}{r}$$

$$V_{ac} = \frac{M_5 - M_7}{rb}$$

$$V_{ab} = \frac{M_4 - M_7}{rc}$$

$$V_a = \frac{M_1 - M_4 - M_5 + M_7}{rbc}$$

From the genetic point of view, the main variance components of interest are those with a strains component, namely V_a, V_{ab}, V_{ac}, and V_{abc}. The derivation of these variances and the environmental variance V_E in terms of observed mean squares, is given in Table 3.2. If values of V_b, V_c, and V_{bc} are required, which represent environmental effects, they can be derived in an analogous way. The value of V_a provides an estimate of the genotypic variance V_G, and hence the heritability can be calculated.

The analysis provides a comprehensive assessment of various genotype × environmental interactions, some of which may be particularly important in behavioural work. To the author's knowledge, no comprehensive experiment of this nature has been carried out for behavioural traits, but it has been used in plant breeding work. However, it is believed that the analysis may find a place in behaviour genetics for a quick survey of the effects of a number of environments on a number of genotypes.

3.4 The components of the genotypic variance

Consider a single locus with two alleles A_1 and A_2. There are three genotypes at the locus A_1A_1, A_1A_2, and A_2A_2. Let us assign genotypic values $-a$, d, and $+a$ to these three genotypes respectively.

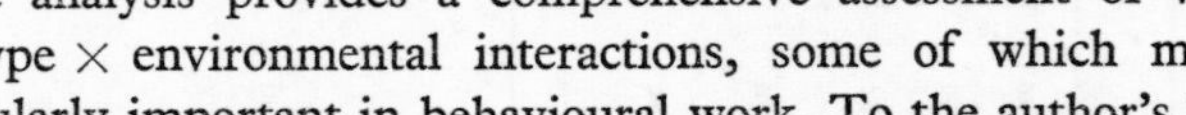

FIG. 3.3 Genotypic values on a linear scale.

We can then represent the genotypes on a linear scale (Fig. 3.3). The zero point is equidistant between the two homozygotes. The value of the heterozygote, d, is positive if A_2 is dominant over A_1, negative if A_1 is dominant over A_2, and if there is no dominance, $d = 0$. Alternatively, if there is no dominance the genotypic values are such that

$$A_1A_2 = \tfrac{1}{2}(A_1A_1 + A_2A_2) = 0 \qquad (3.10)$$

We wish to be able to assess the relative contribution of genes with purely additive effects, represented by a straight line relationship between the number of A_2 genes and the genotypic values (Fig. 3.4), and genes showing dominance which will be represented by the deviation of the genotypic value of A_1A_2 from the straight line relationship between A_1A_1 and A_2A_2 given in Fig. 3.4.

As well as dominance at a particular locus, there may be epistasis, or gene interactions, between loci. Taking these components of the

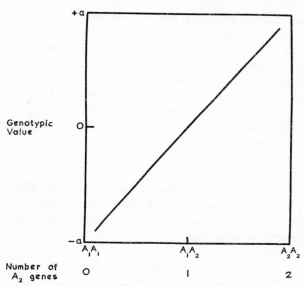

FIG. 3.4 The genotypic values of the three genotypes A_1A_1, A_1A_2, and A_2A_2 plotted against the number of A_2 genes assuming no dominance. Dominance is represented by the deviation of the genotypic value of A_1A_2 from the straight line joining A_1A_1 and A_2A_2.

genotypic value into account, and assuming no genotype × environmental interactions, we can write the genotypic variance as

$$V_G = V_A + V_D + V_I \qquad (3.11)$$

where $V_A =$ variance due to additive genes (additive genetic variance), $V_D =$ variance due to dominance deviations (dominance variance), and $V_I =$ variance due to epistatic interactions (epistatic variance), so that

$$V_P = V_A + V_D + V_I + V_E \qquad (3.12)$$

Some experimental methods enable estimates to be made of all these components. Partly for simplicity we will largely ignore V_I. Furthermore, where estimated, V_A and V_D are usually larger, however, most work is based on morphological traits, and certain behavioural traits could possibly present a different picture.

The ratio of the additive genetic variance to the total variance V_A/V_P can then be computed. It is referred to as the '*heritability in the narrow sense*', $h^2{}_N$. It is a measure of the variation due to additive genes. This is more useful than the heritability in the broad sense defined previously as V_G/V_P, because when considering relationships between generations, it is the gametes carrying genes rather than genotypes that are passed on from one generation to the next. Thus from the predictive point of view, the ratio V_A/V_P is more useful. Designs will now be discussed where V_G can be split into the components V_A and V_D.

3.5 Crosses between two inbred strains

Let us say that we have a cross between two homozygous inbred strains, which we can refer to as parental strains P_1 and P_2. If there is no dominance, from equation 3.10, the F_1 value should be equal to the mid-parental value, thus

$$\frac{P_1 + P_2}{2} = \frac{A_1A_1 + A_2A_2}{2}, \qquad (3.13)$$

which equals 0 in terms of the genotypic values (Fig. 3.3). If the F_1 value $\neq$ 0, then there is dominance, since the genotypic value of the F_1 (A_1A_2) will differ from 0 by an amount d. Thus the F_1 value $= d$, which can be positive or negative according to which parent is dominant. If $d > a$, that is $d/a > 1$, then there will be heterosis or overdominance, since the genotypic value of the heterozygote will be greater than both homozygotes.

Thus the presence of dominance and overdominance can be inferred in a cross between two inbred (homozygous) strains by the relative positions of P_1, P_2, and F_1 on a linear scale of the type given in Fig. 3.3. This leads immediately to an extremely important and theoretically extremely difficult matter to deal with, because the degree of dominance (and overdominance) may depend on the *scale* on which the measurements are made. In Table 3.3 are three sets of hypothetical values for the P_1, P_2, and F_1 generations. The first set is in the scale in which the observations were taken, the second is after

TABLE 3.3   The effect of scale transformations
(After Bruell, 1962)

Scale	P_1	P_2	F_1	d	B_1	B_2	F_2
Raw score	4·00	36·00	16·00	−4·00	8·00	24·00	13·80
Square root	2·00	6·00	4·00	0·00	2·83	4·90	3·71
Logarithmic	0·60	1·56	1·20	0·12	0·90	1·38	1·14

taking square roots, and the third after taking logarithms. In the first case $d < 0$, in the second $d = 0$, and in the third $d > 0$. Thus interpretations could differ according to the scale on which measurements are made.

The problem of scaling has not been satisfactorily resolved, however, Mather (1949) has set up some scaling criteria based on relationships between certain generations. If we have the phenotypic values of P_1, P_2, F_1, B_1 the backcross of the F_1 to the parent P_1 ($P_1 \times F_1$), B_2 the backcross of the F_1 to the parent P_2 ($P_2 \times F_1$), and the F_2, which is the cross between F_1 individuals, then certain scaling criteria can be set up. Whereas the P_1, P_2, and F_1 generations are non-segregating, the B_1, B_2, and F_2 generations are. Thus we obtain

$$B_1 = \frac{P_1 + F_1}{2} = \frac{-a + d}{2}, \qquad (3.14)$$

$$B_2 = \frac{P_2 + F_1}{2} = \frac{a + d}{2}, \qquad (3.15)$$

$$\text{and } F_2 = \frac{P_1 + 2F_1 + P_2}{4} = \frac{-a + 2d + a}{4} = \frac{d}{2} \qquad (3.16)$$

These can be rewritten:

$$\left.\begin{array}{l} 2B_1 - P_1 - F_1 = 0 \ldots A \\ 2B_2 - P_2 - F_1 = 0 \ldots B \\ 4F_2 - 2F_1 - P_1 - P_2 = 0 \ldots C \end{array}\right\} \qquad (3.17)$$

D

The variances of A, B, and C can be easily derived using methods given in elementary statistics texts, and turn out to be

$$
\left.
\begin{aligned}
V_A &= 4V_{B1} + V_{P1} + V_{F1} \\
V_B &= 4V_{B2} + V_{P2} + V_{F1} \\
V_C &= 16V_{F2} + 4V_{F1} + V_{P1} + V_{P2}
\end{aligned}
\right\}
\qquad (3.18)
$$

These variances can then be used in tests of significance to see if A, B, and C differ significantly from 0.

Using the hypothetical values in Table 3.3, it can be shown by substitution in equations 3.17 that the scaling criteria are satisfied only by the logarithmic scale. Thus before carrying out any calculations on the importance of genotype and environment, tests for the adequacy of the scale must be carried out, and if found to be inadequate, a search should be made for a more suitable scale. The process of searching for a scale is rather arbitrary, and in fact this is one of the most awkward problems to deal with in biometrical genetics. In some cases it is difficult or impossible to find a suitable scale, so that genetical interpretations become difficult. Cavalli (1952) has devised a joint scaling test based on the three equations 3.17 combined together. If after carrying out various transformations, the joint scaling test is still significant, then the explanation may lie in the occurrence of non-allelic interactions (epistasis), since the tests all assume the absence of such interactions.

Models have been set up by some authors for estimating non-allelic interactions. Thus considering two loci, there are three possible non-allelic interactions, namely additive $\times$ additive, additive $\times$ dominance, and dominance $\times$ dominance. Such components have been estimated for behavioural traits by Broadhurst and Jinks (1961), where the various formulae involved are summarized.

A second scaling criterion is that the variances must be independent of the means in the non-segregating generations or

$$
V_{P1} = V_{P2} = V_{F1} = V_E \qquad (3.19)
$$

The phenotypic variance can be written as in equation 3.5 thus

$$
V_P = V_G + V_E + 2\mathrm{Cov}_{G,\,E}, \qquad (3.20)
$$

where V_P, V_G, and V_E are the phenotypic, genotypic, and environmental variances respectively, and $\text{Cov}_{G,E}$ is the covariance of genotypic values and environmental deviations. Within each of the generations P_1, P_2, and F_1, $V_G = 0$ by definition, so that the observed phenotypic variance V_P in equation 3.20 must consist of V_E and perhaps $\text{Cov}_{G,E}$. Essentially the criterion that the variances must be independent of the generation means implies that $\text{Cov}_{G,E} = 0$. For behavioural traits, which are often very sensitive to the environment, this criterion may be more difficult to satisfy than for less environment sensitive morphological traits, but further experimental evidence is needed on this point. The criterion that V_{P1}, V_{P2}, and V_{F1} do not depend on the means of P_1, P_2, and F_1, can often be satisfied by a suitable transformation, for example, if the variance is proportional to the mean a logarithmic transformation can be used, and if the data consist of proportions out of a given total or percentages, the angular transformation (Section 3.6) can be used.

In general, when scaling is not satisfactory the main reasons are likely to be:

(1) gene interactions remain, and/or
(2) interactions between genotype and environment remain.

Since a basic aim of biometrical genetics is to ascertain the components of the phenotypic variance, we must see what variances are associated with the P_1, P_2, F_1, B_1, B_2, and F_1 generations. The F_2 consists of $\frac{1}{4}A_1A_1$, $\frac{1}{2}A_1A_2$, $\frac{1}{4}A_2A_2$. These are exactly the proportions expected in a random mating population where the gene frequencies of A_1 and $A_2 = \frac{1}{2}$. In a random mating population it can be shown (Falconer, 1960), that

$$V_P = V_A + V_D + V_E \qquad (3.21)$$

(ignoring for convenience V_I – see equation 3.12). This, then, is the F_2 variance. It can also be shown that

$$V_{B1} + V_{B2} = V_A + 2V_D + 2V_E \qquad (3.22)$$

If the variances of the non-segregating generations are similar, we can use the average variances of these generations to compute V_E thus

$$V_E = \frac{V_{P1} + V_{P2} + V_{F1}}{3} \tag{3.23}$$

As pointed out above, a transformation may be necessary for the variances of the non-segregating generations to become similar. If the sample sizes in these three generations differ, a weighted average of the variances can be used. Thus we can estimate

$$\left.\begin{array}{l} V_A = 2V_{F2} - (V_{B1} + V_{B2}) \\ V_D = V_{F2} - V_A - V_E \end{array}\right\} \tag{3.24}$$

and hence it is possible to compute the heritability.

Example. Broadhurst and Jinks (1961) summarized various experiments applying these methods and some will be discussed in this book. Dawson (1932) tested the inheritance of wildness in mice, defining wildness in terms of the speed the animals showed in running down a straight runway. A movable partition was used by the experimenter to prevent the mouse from running backwards. This introduces a subjective factor, so from the purely psychological point of view the experiment leaves much to be desired, however, it illustrates the genetic points. Two strains, wild and tame, were used which although not highly inbred were very different, so it is reasonable to see to what extent and how the differences are controlled genetically. The means and standard errors as used in the analysis are given in Table 3.4. Cavalli's (1952) joint scaling test gave a probability

TABLE 3.4   Data of Dawson (1932) for running speed in mice (seconds)

(After Broadhurst and Jinks, 1961)

Generation	P$_1$ (wild)	P$_2$ (tame)	F$_1$	F$_2$	B$_1$	B$_2$
Males	6·7 ± 0·3	24·5 ± 1·0	7·6 ± 0·3	13·0 ± 0·6	6·6 ± 0·3	20·8 ± 1·6
Females	5·3 ± 0·3	25·3 ± 1·2	6·9 ± 0·3	11·8 ± 0·5	6·2 ± 0·5	18·7 ± 1·5
Both	5·9 ± 0·2	24·9 ± 0·8	7·2 ± 0·2	12·4 ± 0·4	6·4 ± 0·4	19·7 ± 1·4

of between 0·05 and 0·02 for goodness of fit between observed and expected. The P$_1$, P$_2$, and F$_1$ variances were not entirely homogeneous, and so the square root and log transformations were tried. The log scale was the most satisfactory, giving for Cavalli's scaling test a probability of > 0.90 for goodness of fit. Variances were estimated after taking logs thus

$$V_A = 0.026 \pm 0.012$$
$$V_D = 0.002 \pm 0.008$$
$$V_E = 0.020 \pm 0.005,$$

giving
$$h^2_N = \frac{0.026}{0.044} = 0.59$$

On the linear scale it was found that the additive $\times$ dominance interaction component was largely responsible for the non-allelic interactions. In fact, of the examples analysed by Broadhurst and Jinks (1961), most showed this type of non-allelic interaction.

3.6 *Diallel crosses*

A diallel cross is the set of all possible matings between several strains or genotypes, thus for four strains there are sixteen possible combinations:

		Strain of male parent			
		A	B	C	D
Strain of female parent	A	AA	AB	AC	AD
	B	BA	BB	BC	BD
	C	CA	CB	CC	CD
	D	DA	DB	DC	DD

made up of six crosses AB, AC, AD, BC, BD, and CD, their six reciprocals BA, CA, DA, CB, DB, and DC, where the sex of the parents is transposed, and four kinds of offspring derived from the four parental strains AA, BB, CC, and DD which are arranged along the leading diagonal. In general, if there are n strains, the diallel table will have n^2 entries made up of $\frac{n(n-1)}{2}$ crosses, $\frac{n(n-1)}{2}$ reciprocals and n parental strains. Diallel crossing techniques vary depending on whether the parental strains or the reciprocal F_1s are included, or both. There are four possible experimental methods:

(1) parents, one set of F_1s and reciprocal F_1s are included (all n^2 combinations);

(2) parents and one set of F_1s, but not the reciprocal F_1s are included ($\frac{1}{2}n(n+1)$ combinations);

(3) one set of F_1s and reciprocals are included but not the parents ($n(n-1)$ combinations), and

(4) one set of F_1s, but neither the parents nor the reciprocal F_1s are included ($\frac{1}{2}n(n-1)$ combinations).

There are a variety of theoretical methods of analysis of diallel crosses, depending somewhat on the information required (see, for example, Mather, 1949; Hayman, 1958; Griffing, 1956; Kempthorne, 1957; Wearden, 1964). One of the first detailed genetic analyses of a diallel cross for a behavioural trait (Broadhurst, 1960, and Section 4.2) was carried out on six strains of rats for defecation scores (number of fecal boluses deposited in an arena in exactly two minutes) and ambulation scores (number of marked areas entered in the arena in exactly two minutes), using the analytical methods of Mather (1949) and his colleagues. It is neither possible nor desirable to review all the methods for analysing diallel crosses and the information that they provide. In this book, the type of information that can be obtained from the diallel cross will be discussed in the framework of Griffing's (1956) presentation, which by a relatively simple analysis of variance yields information on the additive, dominance, and environmental components of variance of a trait. As for the previous methods of analysis, the validity of the estimates of the variance components depends on the strains being assumed to be a random sample from some population about which inferences are to be made. However, in some cases we cannot assume this as the strains may be deliberately chosen and so the experimental material then constitutes the entire population about which inferences can be made.

To examine the type of information that can be obtained, we will discuss a 6×6 diallel cross for mating speed in *Drosophila melanogaster* made up of six inbred strains that had been sib-mated for at least 120 generations at the time of the experiment, the fifteen possible hybrids between the inbred strains and the fifteen reciprocal hybrids (Parsons, 1964). Males and females were stored separately at eclosion, and at six days of age a single male was shaken in with a female and observed until copulation began. The time in minutes for this to occur is the mating speed. Pairs not mating in $\leqslant 40$ minutes were recorded as unmated. For each of the thirty-six

TABLE 3.5   Mean numbers of successful matings out of seven
in forty minutes in *D. melanogaster*

(After Parsons, 1964)

		Strain of ♂ parent					
		N1	N2	Y1	Y2	G5	OR
	N1	*4·5*	5	6	0·5	6	7
	N2	6	*6·5*	5·5	5	6	7
Strain of	Y1	6·5	7	*2·5*	6	4·5	6·5
♀ parent	Y2	2·5	6·5	4·5	*0·5*	7	7
	G5	5·5	5	5	3	*6·5*	7
	OR	7	6	6·5	6	6	*3·5*

possible combinations, fourteen trials were carried out split into two
replicates of seven. In Table 3.5 the mean numbers mating out of
seven trials are given for those mating in forty minutes. The means
for the inbred strains are in italics. In Table 3.6 the means of the

TABLE 3.6   Mean numbers of successful matings for hybrids
(X_i. and $X._i$) and inbred strains X_{ii} in *D. melanogaster*

(After Parsons, 1964)

Strain	Time period								
	⩽10 minutes			⩽20 minutes			⩽40 minutes*		
	$X_i.$	$X._i$	X_{ii}	$X_i.$	$X._i$	X_{ii}	$X_i.$	$X._i$	X_{ii}
N1	2·4	3·5	1·5	3·1	4·7	2	4·9	5·5	4·5
N2	2·9	3·5	4·5	4·4	4·6	5	5·9	5·9	6·5
Y1	4·1	2·6	2	5	3·7	2	6·1	5·5	2·5
Y2	3·9	2·4	0·5	4·9	3·2	0·5	5·5	4·1	0·5
G5	2·7	3·6	1·5	3·9	4·5	3·5	5·1	5·9	6·5
OR	5·2	5·6	1	6	6·6	2	6·3	6·9	3·5
Overall mean	3·53		1·83	4·55		2·5	5·63		4

* Based on the data in Table 3.5.

females of a given strain with the five other strains $X_i.$, and the means
of the males of a given strain with the five other strains $X._i$ are
given. The means for the inbred strains themselves X_{ii} are also
given. Results are presented for 3 time intervals, namely those mating
in ⩽ 10, ⩽ 20, and ⩽ 40 minutes. There is significant hybrid

vigour comparing the inbreds and hybrids especially for the $\leqslant$ 10 minute data. In Section 6.2, the common occurrence of hybrid vigour for behavioural traits in rodents will be noted.

Before carrying out analyses of variance, it is necessary to transform the data. The data consist of percentages or proportions of successful matings after a given time period. Let p = proportion of successful matings and q = proportion of unsuccessful matings such that $p + q = 1$, then for this binomial situation it is well known that the variance of p

$$V_p = \frac{pq}{n} = V_q, \tag{3.25}$$

so that the variance depends on the mean p. If, however, the angular transformation (Fisher, 1949)

$$p = \sin^2 \phi \tag{3.26}$$

is applied, where ϕ is an angle in radians from $0°$ to $90°$, then the variance of ϕ can be shown to be

$$\tfrac{1}{4}n, \tag{3.27}$$

which is independent of the mean and depends only on the sample size (n) on which an observation is based. This change of scale removes correlations between the means and variances.

Using the method in Section 3.3, the analysis of variance on the transformed proportions of matings for the inbred strains themselves gave differences between strains significant at the $0\cdot1\%$ level for the $\leqslant$ 10 minute data, and at the 1% level for the $\leqslant$ 20 and $\leqslant$ 40 minute data. Heritabilities in the broad sense h^2_B came to $0\cdot81$, $0\cdot73$, and $0\cdot75$ for the three time periods respectively. Thus there are substantial differences between the inbred strains in mating speed. Estimates of V_A and V_D cannot be obtained from the inbred strains (Section 3.3) but can be obtained from the hybrids. The further analysis of the diallel cross will be based on the hybrids without the inbred strains, because Griffing (1956) has shown that to obtain unbiassed estimates of V_A and V_D the inbred strains should be omitted.

Based on Table 3.6, an overall idea of a given strain in hybrid combination with all the other strains will be given by $X_{i.} + X._i$ which comes to 5·9 for the $\leqslant$10 minute data for strain N1, and 10·8 for strain OR. The average mating speed of a given strain in hybrid combination, obtained by considering all possible hybrids of that strain, is referred to as the *general combining ability* (g.c.a.) of that strain. Normally, general combining abilities are expressed as deviations from the overall population mean. In any case, it is clear that the g.c.a. of strain N1 < strain OR.

Given the general combining abilities of two strains, say N1 and OR, it is possible to predict an expected average mating speed of the crosses between N1 and OR, that is for N1♀ × OR ♂ and its reciprocal. The degree to which the mating speed of this cross differs from that predicted on the basis of the general combining abilities of N1 and OR is referred to as the *specific combining ability* (s.c.a.). Finally, it is possible to calculate the degree to which N1 ♀ × OR ♂ differs from its reciprocal OR ♀ × N1 ♂. This is referred to as a

TABLE 3.7 Analysis of variance of the diallel cross of hybrids for the mean number of successful matings in *D. melanogaster*

				Time Period			
		$\leqslant$10 minutes		$\leqslant$20 minutes		$\leqslant$40 minutes	
Model I	d.f.	M.S.	F	M.S.	F	M.S.	F
G.c.a.	5	2,554·8	13·42‡	2,547·5	16·94‡	1,499·4	9·51‡
S.c.a.	9	504·1	3·04*	724·9	4·82‡	654·2	4·15†
Reciprocal	15	499·6	3·02†	535·0	3·56†	415·2	2·63*
Error	30	165·7		150·4		157·6	
Model II							
G.c.a.		5·07*		3·51*		2·29	
		The F values for s.c.a. and reciprocal effects are as in Model I.					
Components of variance (Model II)							
V_A		256		228		106	
V_D		85		144		124	
V_E		166		150		158	
h^2_N		0·51		0·44		0·27	

* $p < 0.05$ † $p < 0.01$.   ‡ $p < 0.001$.

reciprocal effect. The next stage is to carry out an analysis of variance for these various effects.

In Table 3.7 the results of the analyses of variance are given for the proportions mating in $\leqslant$ 10, $\leqslant$ 20, and $\leqslant$ 40 minutes, showing highly significant g.c.a.'s for all time periods, while the s.c.a.s and reciprocal effects are significant but at a lower level (see F values for model I). As might be expected from Table 3.6, strain N1 has a significantly positive g.c.a. and strains Y2 and OR significantly negative g.c.a.s. A positive g.c.a. means that the mating speed of the strain in hybrid combination is faster than the population mean mating speed, while a negative g.c.a. means that the mating speed of the strain in hybrid combination is slower than the population mean. A significant s.c.a. means that the particular hybrid combination between two strains mates significantly faster or slower than would be predicted from the g.c.a.s of the strains making up the hybrid. Various s.c.a.s were significant, the most significant being a negative s.c.a. for the hybrid between N1 and Y2. Some significant reciprocal differences were also found.

It is also possible to estimate the g.c.a. variance, $V_{g.c.a.}$, the s.c.a. variance, $V_{s.c.a.}$, the reciprocal variance, V_r, and the environmental variance, V_E. Now under the model described so far, where we were testing for differences between the inbred strains expressed as combining abilities and reciprocal effects, all the F tests were based on the error M.S. (model I). When testing the significance of the variances given above, the same F tests apply for $V_{s.c.a.}$ and V_r, but the significance of $V_{g.c.a.}$ must be tested by the ratio of

$$\frac{\text{M.S. for g.c.a.}}{\text{M.S. for s.c.a.}} \text{ (model II – Table 3.7),}$$

because of the nature of the expected mean squares (Griffing, 1956). Model I thus deals with differences between means and model II with relative magnitude of variances.

Now considering model II, since the g.c.a. of a strain represents its overall mating speed in hybrid combination, it will essentially represent additive gene effects. It can, in fact, be shown that

$$2V_{g.c.a.} = V_A \qquad (3.28)$$

The s.c.a. variance, $V_{s.c.a.}$, due to the deviations of specific crosses between pairs of strains from the g.c.a.s of the same pair of strains, is a measure of dominance, and it can be shown that

$$V_{s.c.a.} = V_D \text{ (Griffing, 1956)} \qquad (3.29)$$

The validity of the estimates V_A, V_D, and V_E depends, as mentioned previously, on the strains being assumed to be a random sample from a population about which inferences are to be made. This condition is probably fulfilled reasonably in the experiment being discussed. For $V_{g.c.a.}$, F decreases from the $\leqslant$ 10 to the $\leqslant$ 40 minute group of data showing that the relative importance of additive genes declines with time. This is reflected in a progressive reduction in V_A with time, which is countered by an increase in V_D at least between ten and twenty minutes. V_E is very similar for each time period, showing that the environmental component of variance is independent of the means which indicates that the angular transformation is successful. The decline of V_A with time is reflected in a decline of h^2_N.

Initially, therefore, it seems that the behaviour of strains in hybrid combination (that is, g.c.a. effects) is important as this contributes to V_A. However, at a later stage the performance of specific crosses and hence of specific gene combinations begins to become more important, for this will contribute to V_D. Perhaps somewhat different genes are important at different times, or alternatively, the dominance relations of the same genes change with time.

This analysis, therefore, reveals that there is a strong genotypic component in mating speed. This is hardly surprising, for as already indicated, it is an important component of fitness and will play a part in determining which flies will most readily transmit genes to subsequent generations.

The diallel technique has a further application. Instead of breeding the F_1s, we may wish to know what happens when studying mating behaviour between combinations of strains. Thus, for example, we can ask whether the genotype of the male or female is more important in determining mating speed for a series of time periods. We can illustrate this using the *D. pseudoobscura* data discussed in Section 2.4 for the nine possible combinations between the three karyotypes ST/ST, ST/CH, and CH/CH. In Table 2·3 the frequencies mating out of fifty in five minutes are given. It is clear by inspection that the marginal totals for males are more variable than for females, and this is confirmed by an analysis of variance separating out variation due to female and male karyotypes (Table 3.8). Furthermore, since the data are in the form of a 3 × 3 diallel cross, it is possible to carry out an analysis of variance for combining abilities. The model used is slightly different from that just discussed, because a component for paternal effects is included in view of the very much greater contribution of the karyotype of the males

TABLE 3.8   Analysis of variance of the number mating out of fifty in five minutes after applying the angular transformation in *D. pseudoobscura*

(After Kaul and Parsons, 1965)

Source of variation	d.f.	M.S.	F	P
Female karyotypes	2	11·5	0·36	
Male karyotypes	2	412·0	12·84	$P < 0.01$
Replicates (crowding levels)	1	175·5	5·47	$P < 0.05$
Error	12	32·1		

than the females in determining mating speed. The model is given by Wearden (1964), and in this case the three combinations of karyotypes mating with themselves are included, since it is not meaningful to estimate variance components.

The combining ability analysis confirmed that the mating speed varied between karyotypes, and that the differences were controlled mainly by the karyotype of the males. The specific combining ability component is of particular interest, since it measures interactions between karyotypes in a behavioural sense, but this was not significant. Rather similar conclusions were arrived at for the duration of copulation, and in *D. melanogaster* a 5 × 5 diallel cross for various combinations between inbred strains gave analogous results for mating speed (Parsons, 1965 *a*).

It must not be thought that the genotype of the male always determines mating speed (see also Section 2.4). In fact, in one experiment Parsons and Kaul (1966 *a*) studied mating speeds for a 3 × 3 table for the karyotypic combinations AR/AR, AR/PP, and PP/PP (AR = Arrowhead, and PP = Pikes Peak) in *D. pseudoobscura*, and found the female to be more important than the male. In some of the diallel crosses carried out for mating speed, the relative importance of the genotype of the female increases with time when, presumably, the female's reaction to the male's courtship becomes important. This trend can, of course, be assessed by carrying out the analysis after a series of time periods. For duration of copulation, however, the genotype of the male seems to be more important in general, presumably because copulation ceases when the sperm have been transferred.

The experiment of Parsons and Kaul (1966 a) was carried out at two temperatures 20° C and 25° C, and substantial genotype × environmental interactions were found such that there was more change between temperatures for the homokaryotypes than the heterokaryotypes. Thus the heterokaryotypes show more *behavioural homeostasis* between environments than the homokaryotypes. Analogous results have been found for many fitness factors in many species, for example, in *D. pseudoobscura* Dobzhansky and Levene (1955) showed that the viabilities of homozygotes of nineteen different second chromosomes were more variable under a series of environments than the heterozygotes. Parsons (1959) presented similar results for larval survival in *D. melanogaster* (see also Langridge, 1962). Thus mating speed seems to show at least some of the properties of the various more classical components of fitness studied in *Drosophila* (see also Chapter Eight).

The diallel cross technique can thus be used for estimating the variance components of behavioural traits, and for studying behaviour itself for combinations of various strains. It is a powerful technique for a general survey of a series of strains, perhaps in several different environments, whatever the aim or model used. It has the advantage that a single generation provides a great deal of information. Although some additional information can come from further generations, the present state of behavioural sciences does not seem to warrant the additional labour in view of the comparatively small additional amount of information obtainable. For behavioural traits where genotype × environmental interactions may be important, the one generation approach has clear advantages. The diallel technique is an extensive analytical method rather than intensive, as a number of strains and hybrids can be surveyed at once. It seems to represent an eminently suitable first technique in an investigation of a behavioural trait in an organism where adequate inbred strains exist.

3.7 Relationships between relatives

We do not have a ready supply of inbred strains in all organisms. This applies especially to higher organisms, including man. The method that can be used under these circumstances is the calculation of variance components and heritabilities from an analysis of correlations between relatives. In the treatment of the resemblance between relatives we assume the parents to be a random sample of their generation and to be mated at random.

We will not here give the derivations of formulae for correlations between relatives, since they are fully discussed in Falconer (1960) and other texts. It is not difficult, however, to visualize that half of the genes of any offspring will be common with a given parent and half

TABLE 3.9   Correlations between relatives

Relatives	Covariance between relatives	Correlation coefficient
Monozygotic twin	$V_A + V_D$	$> h^2_N$
Mid-parent, child	$\frac{1}{2}V_A$	$\dfrac{h^2_N}{\sqrt{2}}$
Parent, child	$\frac{1}{2}V_A$	$\frac{1}{2}h^2_N$
Sib, sib $\left.\right\}$ Dizygotic twin	$\frac{1}{2}V_A + \frac{1}{4}V_D$	$> \frac{1}{2}h^2_N$
Half sibs $\left.\right\}$ Uncle, nephew Aunt, niece	$\frac{1}{4}V_A$	$\frac{1}{4}h^2_N$
First cousin	$\frac{1}{8}V_A$	$\frac{1}{8}h^2_N$
Second cousin	$\frac{1}{32}V_A$	$\frac{1}{32}h^2_N$

will be different. Thus of the additive variance, V_A, in the parents half will go to the offspring, so that the covariance between parent and offspring $= \frac{1}{2} V_A$ (Table 3.9). Now since the phenotypic variance V_P, in the parental and offspring generations can be assumed to be the same, the correlation coefficient between parent and offspring

$$r_{OP} = \frac{\frac{1}{2}V_A}{\sqrt{(V_P . V_P)}} = \frac{1}{2}h^2_N \qquad (3.30)$$

Full sibs will have half of their additive genes in common as in the above situation. However, because they have two parents in common, they may have some genotypes in common, so that the covariance between sibs includes a dominance component. It turns out to be

$$\tfrac{1}{2}V_A + \tfrac{1}{4}V_D \tag{3.31}$$

Because of the dominance component, the correlation coefficient between full sibs

$$\frac{\tfrac{1}{2}V_A + \tfrac{1}{4}D}{V_P} \tag{3.32}$$

will slightly overestimate $\tfrac{1}{2}h^2{}_N$ (Table 3.9). The same formulae apply to dizygotic twins, but the heritability could be further inflated because of the common environment of twins.

The covariance between monozygotic twins is merely the total genotypic variance since all genotypes are in common, but heritability estimates are again likely to be inflated because of the common environment between twin pairs (Table 3.9). Further discussions on twins in behaviour genetics research in man will be deferred to Chapter Seven.

Various other covariances between relatives and correlation coefficients are given in Table 3.9. For progressively more remote relatives, the contribution of V_A decreases as expected. The correlation coefficients decrease at the same rate (ignoring V_D components), with the exception of the coefficient between mid-parent and child. The reason for this is that, defining the mid-parental variance as $V_{\bar{P}}$, where $\bar{P} = \tfrac{1}{2}(P_1 + P_2)$, and P_1 and P_2 are the values of the two parents, it turns out that

$$V_{\bar{P}} = \tfrac{1}{2}V_P, \tag{3.33}$$

so that the correlation between mid-parent and offspring comes to

$$\frac{V_A}{\sqrt{\left(\dfrac{V_P}{2} \cdot V_P\right)}} = \frac{h^2{}_N}{\sqrt{2}} \tag{3.34}$$

For relationships between parent and offspring a regression approach can also be used. It is well known from work of Galton and Pearson that the sons of tall men tend to be tall, but not as tall as their fathers, yet not as short as the average of the population. In fact, the height of sons tends to go or regress about half-way towards the average of the population. Similarly, the sons of short men tend to be short, but not as short as their fathers, and on average have heights about half-way between their fathers and the population average. This regression by half towards the mean is exactly what we would expect based on additive genes. In fact, if $b_{O\bar{P}}$ is the regression coefficient of offspring on parent, it can be shown that

$$b_{O\bar{P}} = \tfrac{1}{2} \frac{V_A}{V_P} = \frac{h^2_N}{2} = r_{OP},\qquad(3.35)$$

where r_{OP} is the correlation between parent and offspring. The better parent to use is the father, since the regression of offspring on mother may give too high an estimate because of maternal effects. It can also be shown that the regression of offspring on mid-parent, $b_{O\bar{P}}$, is equal to the heritability, h^2_N, or

$$b_{O\bar{P}} = h^2_N.\qquad(3.36)$$

The use of relationships between mid-parent and offspring depends on the variances being equal in both sexes, and so is perhaps less useful than the relationships between one parent and offspring. Furthermore, so far as behaviour is concerned, many traits are sex-limited such as components of sexual behaviour, so that the mid-parent approach would be invalid.

Examples of the application of certain of the methods discussed will be given later in the book, especially in Chapter Seven.

Sometimes the mating of parents is not at random but according to their phenotypic resemblance, a system known as *assortative mating*. There is, then, a correlation between the phenotypic values of the mated pairs. The consequences of assortative mating have not been studied in great detail, and in practice are often ignored or perhaps circumvented by the experimental design, but in situations where mating cannot be controlled, its existence must be remembered. Its importance will depend, among other things, on the heritability of the trait under study. It is merely mentioned here as a possible source of bias, but it will be discussed in further detail at a later stage.

One problem, especially in man, in using correlations between relatives is that of non-genetic factors common to families being confounded with the common portion of their genotype and so leading to inflated estimates of heritability. This applies particularly to methods for correlations between full sibs and for twins. In laboratory experiments these correlations can be held to a minimum. The use of half-sib families which have a common sire but different mothers also helps to minimize these complications.

3.8 *Conclusions*

For a behavioural trait that has not been previously investigated in an organism such as *Drosophila*, where plenty of inbred strains are available, a first experiment might be a study of the strains themselves in a series of environments to obtain an idea of the heritability of the trait in the broad sense, followed by a diallel cross in a few of the critical environments. According to the results obtained at this stage, it may or may not be worth proceeding to the three-generation system of P_1, P_2, F_1, F_2, B_1, and B_2. For this three-generation system, if the parents, P_1 and P_2, can be assumed to be completely homozygous, then in generation 1 the cross $P_1 \times P_2 \to F_1$ could be carried out and the parentals bred again. In generation 2 the crosses $F_1 \times F_1 \to F_2$, $F_1 \times P_1 \to B_1$, $F_1 \times P_2 \to B_2$ could be carried out, a repeat of $P_1 \times P_2 \to F_1$, and the parentals bred for a further generation. Given completely homozygous parents, the genotype of the F_1 in the successive generations should be identical. This means that all the generations P_1, P_2, F_1, F_2, B_1, and B_2 could be surveyed in one generation and so avoid complications due to environmental variations between generations, which certainly seem to occur for indefinable reasons in *Drosophila*. It is also possible to repeat the complete series of crosses in several environments to search for genotype $\times$ environmental interactions of various types. Not all methods based on inbred strains and hybrids have been surveyed, but other suitable designs have been presented in the literature. The greatest present need is for more data, provided that the trait in question can be measured reasonably objectively.

E

The last section of the chapter gave methods of obtaining components of variance from correlations between relatives, which are particularly suitable for organisms such as man where inbred strains do not exist. Although such methods can be used for any animals where random mating occurs (and methods have been devised for situations where there are deviations from random mating), they have not been used extensively in behavioural studies. In man in particular there is the extreme difficulty of separating heredity from environment, which in general does not pose problems in organisms where there are many inbred strains available. Such difficulties will be further discussed in Chapter Seven.

The methods described in this chapter are, of course, merely routine methods of biometrical genetics such as have been used in animal and plant breeding for many years, and which have been adapted to the study of behaviour. The possibility of applying biometrical genetics to behaviour has only recently been appreciated. In the *Drosophila* experiments the work has been concentrated on mating behaviour, which necessarily involves an interaction between two sexes. This is perhaps unfortunate as it could lead to difficulties in the interpretation of variance components and heritabilities if interactions of a behavioural type occur between mating individuals. In the experiments discussed there is little evidence for this, so the variance components and heritabilities are probably reasonably reliable. However, it is to be hoped that there will be work on other behavioural traits in *Drosophila*, using the designs outlined in this chapter in the near future. Some limited work in rodents will be discussed in Chapter Six. In conclusion, methods are available for the analysis of quantitative behavioural traits, and the next few years may well see the accumulation of a considerable amount of experimental data.

CHAPTER FOUR

Selection Experiments

4.1 Introduction

The genetic material can be manipulated by selecting individuals at
the high or low extremes of a distribution for the quantitative trait of
interest, in the hope of forming separate high or low lines in subsequent generations. This is called directional selection (Fig. 4.1). If

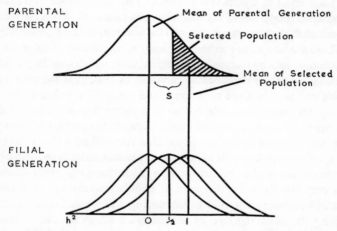

FIG. 4.1 The dependence of the response to directional selection on:
(1) the mean of the selected population; (2) the heritability.

the trait has some genetic basis, there should be a response to selection,
since by selecting extreme phenotypes extreme genotypes will be
selected. At the outset at least, the magnitude of the response, R, to
selection will depend on the heritability (in the narrow sense) and
the selection differential, S, which is the mean phenotypic value of

the individuals selected as parents expressed as a deviation from the mean phenotypic value of all the individuals in the parental generation before selection was made (Fig. 4.1). The magnitude of S depends on two factors, namely the proportion of population included among the selected group, and the standard deviation of the trait (see Falconer, 1960, for a more complete discussion). Provided that fertility and viability are not correlated with the trait under study, the response to selection is then given by

$$R = h^2{}_N S.$$

Clearly, the larger the heritability the greater the response. If $h^2{}_N = 0$, no response to selection is possible, for the trait would be determined entirely by the environment (Fig. 4.1). Theoretically, the prediction of the response is only valid for one generation, because the basic effect of selection is to change gene frequencies, and hence the genetic properties of the offspring generation. However, in many experiments the response is retained for five, ten, or more generations.

There are two main methods for improving the rate of response to selection. One is by increasing the heritability, which may be possible by reducing the environmental variation by care in selecting a trait which can be measured objectively and easily. The other is by reducing the proportion selected so that those that are selected are extremes. There are, however, some limitations to this. One important consideration is that the population size will set a lower limit to the number of individuals to be used as parents, since extremely high numbers may need to be measured to reduce the proportion selected to a very low level. Furthermore, if population sizes are very small this will automatically lead to inbreeding and hence homozygosity, which will reduce the level of variability on which selection can act. Another factor limiting the response is that general fertility and viability frequently decrease during selection. This can be explained by genotypes not previously exposed to the action of natural selection becoming subjected to it. There is a vast literature on selection experiments, and many methods are available depending on the exact objectives, the organism, and its breeding system (see Falconer, 1960).

Since $h^2{}_N$ must be > 0 for a response to selection, it is desirable first to determine the heritability of the trait. This can be done by one of the methods discussed in the previous chapter, or by various other methods as discussed in Falconer (1960) and in other texts.

During the selection process extreme phenotypes are continuously favoured. This, in all likelihood, will lead to an increasing proportion of extreme genotypes which are likely to be homozygous. Ultimately, therefore, the rate of response to selection will be expected to diminish, and perhaps there will be a series of generations where there is no response, that is, the population will be at a plateau. Occasionally, after some generations at a plateau, there is a rapid response for a few generations which is called an 'accelerated response to selection'. To a certain extent these rapid responses have been shown to be repeatable (Thoday and Boam, 1961) in selection experiments for sternopleural chaeta number in *Drosophila melanogaster*. This argues against contamination as a cause, and population sizes are usually far too small in selection experiments to reasonably invoke mutation. The likely interpretation is recombination between linked genes controlling the trait leading to extreme gametes, which then being favoured by selection will increase in frequency rapidly, probably leading to extreme homozygotes, unless the homozygotes are extremely unfit or lethal, as may happen occasionally.

If selection leads to an increased proportion of homozygotes, or at least to a fall in genetic heterogeneity, then there is the possibility of assessing the contribution of each chromosome to the response to selection in organisms such as *Drosophila melanogaster*, where suitable stocks exist to aid in such an analysis. It may be possible to go so far as to identify and locate actual genes responsible, as has been done by Thoday (1961) and his colleagues in analysing the response to selection for sternopleural chaeta number.

In this chapter some of the few experiments which show a response to selection for behavioural traits will be discussed. There is the possibility not only of learning something of the genetic basis of behaviour, but also of learning something of behaviour itself, especially if the behavioural trait under analysis can be divided into components, some of which may be differentially affected by selection.

Early studies showing that responses to selection can be obtained for behavioural traits are reviewed by Broadhurst (1960). Without citing specific references, responses to selection have been found for traits such as susceptibility to audiogenic seizures in rats and mice, running speed in mice, and sex drive, maze learning ability, cage activity, early or late onset of mating, and emotional elimination in rats. Other work showing responses to selection in rodents will be discussed in Chapter Six. The occurrence of responses shows that there are heritable components for these traits, but it is difficult to come to any further conclusions without carrying out additional genetical analyses on the selectively bred strains. Broadhurst (1960) does, however, mention that in the case of maze learning, cage activity, and emotional elimination in rats some further crosses were made. In all cases F_1s were obtained, for maze learning F_2s also, and for cage activity F_2, B_1, and B_2 generations. These crosses provided some information on the genetic control of the traits. For example, Brody (1942) who worked on cage activity, claimed that she had detected a major gene pair responsible with modifier genes. In general, however, little information of a genetic nature has emerged from these early selection experiments. The one conclusion that can be made is that the responses to selection imply a positive heritability and hence a component of additive genetic variance, assuming extra-chromosomal inheritance to be unimportant.

4.2 Defecation and ambulation scores in rats

Broadhurst (1960) carried out a selective breeding experiment for ten generations for the defecation score in rats, which in his experiments is defined as the number of faecal boluses deposited in an arena in exactly two minutes. He established a high and a low line which diverged rapidly (Fig. 4.2). The lines were maintained by brother–sister matings. The rapid response is hardly surprising, since a diallel cross between six strains of pure-bred rats gave the high heritability h^2_N of 0·62 for the defecation score. Based on the selectively bred reactive line P_1 (high defecation score) and the non-reactive line P_2 (low defecation score) at the eighth generation of selection, F_1, F_2, B_1, and B_2 generations were bred and the heritability h^2_N obtained was 0·95, which is exceedingly high and is considered by Broadhurst to be an overestimate. The computation of the

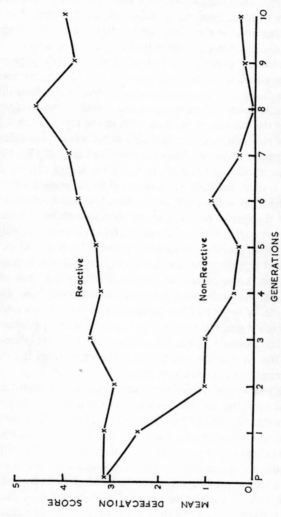

FIG. 4.2 Results of selective breeding for high and low defecation scores over ten generations. The ordinate shows the mean number of faecal boluses deposited per trial. (After Broadhurst, 1960.)

estimate is, however, based on the assumption that the lines P_1 and P_2 are homozygous, which would be a source of error since homozygosity after eight generations would hardly be complete. For this reason and also because the diallel cross surveys a greater range of parents, the diallel cross estimate is probably more realistic.

In any selection experiment it is desirable to study possible correlated responses to selection. These will provide information on behaviour itself, as well as on its genetic control. Thus Broadhurst obtained simultaneous information on the ambulation score, which he defined as the number of marked areas in the arena entered by a rat in exactly two minutes. The ambulation scores corresponding to the reactive and non-reactive lines are given in Fig. 4.3. There is an increase in the mean score of both lines, but the increase in the non-reactive line is more marked. Thus selection for defecation score has a marked effect on a trait not under direct selection. Broadhurst suggests that the similar response to selection in both lines might be due partly to a variable such as inbreeding which operates equally on both lines. To investigate the situation more fully it would be desirable to select separately for the two traits in two different populations, and observe the correlated responses for the trait not under direct selection. For ambulation score the diallel cross above gave a heritability h^2_N of 0·89, and the heritability using the two selected lines at the eighth generation and the F_1, F_2, B_1, and B_2 generations from these lines came to 0·80. Both values are reasonably close to each other, but for reasons cited earlier, the value from the diallel cross is believed to be more accurate.

This work is of considerable importance, since it demonstrates the feasibility of applying the methods of biometrical genetics to behaviour in mammals, and in fact represents one of the first comprehensive attempts to apply the methods of biometrical genetics to quantitative behavioural traits in any organism. Even so, it is difficult to take the analysis much farther. Given a response to selection and substantial additive genetic variance, the next stage is to find out whether the genetic activity so revealed is distributed at random throughout the genome, or whether it is restricted to a few chromosomes. It is very difficult to answer this type of question in mammals. For this reason we will now turn to some experiments in *Drosophila*,

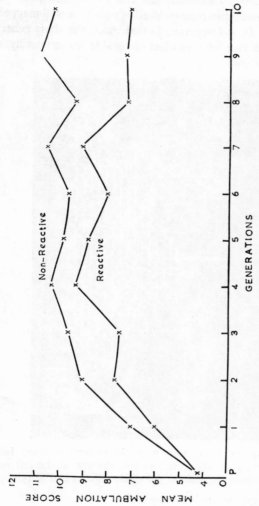

FIG. 4.3 Results of selective breeding for high and low defecation scores over ten generations. The graph shows the correlated response of the mean ambulation score, measured as the average number of metres run per trial. (After Broadhurst, 1960.)

where much more refined genetic analyses are possible, because of the stocks available. *Drosophila* also has the advantage of having fewer chromosomes than mammals, all of which are well mapped in a species such as *D. melanogaster*. Furthermore, the short generation time and rapid rate of reproduction enable an extremely rapid accumulation of data.

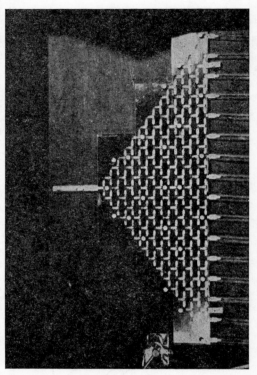

FIG. 4.4 Photograph of 15-unit maze in vertical position facing a fluorescent tube. Flies are introduced in the vial at the left and are collected from the vials at the right. (After Hirsch, 1963.)

4.3 *Selection experiments in Drosophila*

Hirsch (1963) has carried out a reasonably detailed analysis of the relationship between the genome and a behavioural phenotype in studies of geotaxis (gravity orientated locomotion) using a vertical

15-unit plastic maze (Fig. 4.4). Flies are introduced on the left hand side of the maze and are collected from one of the vials on the right. They are attracted through the maze by the odour of food, and by lighting in the form of a fluorescent tube on the right-hand side. The apparatus permits the screening of the behaviour of a large number of flies with the exclusion of human handling once the flies have been introduced, so conditions for maximum objectivity are provided. Selection for positive and negative geotaxis produced a rapid and clear response (Fig. 4.5).

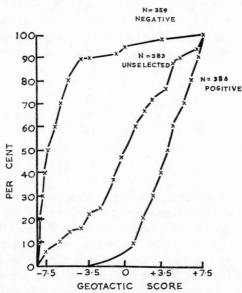

FIG. 4.5 Cumulative percentages of flies (males and females) for various geotactic scores in a fifteen-unit maze, for an unselected foundation population and two selected lines. (After Hirsch, 1963.)

Erlenmeyer-Kimling assayed the role of the three major chromosomes of *D. melanogaster* in the response to selection for geotaxis using methods described by Mather (1942) and Mather and Harrison (1949) in chaeta number selection experiments (see Hirsch 1962). The procedure consists of taking a multiple tester stock, for example,

$$A/+, B/C, D/E$$

where A, B, C, D, and E, are dominant markers on the X, II, and III chromosomes respectively. The presence of inversions in the tester chromosomes prevents crossing-over in heterozygotes, so that they segregate to all intents and purposes as whole units. Females of this stock are crossed to males of the line to be assayed, giving females of the type

A/S, B/S, D/S

where S represents the selection line to be assayed. These females are then backcrossed to the selection line under analysis. Assuming markers A, B, and D to be associated with inversions, the S chromosomes in the above females will be broken down very little by recombination, and thus they will go to the next generation relatively intact. In the backcross there are eight classes of progeny, namely,

(1) A   B   D
(2) A   B
(3) A   D
(4) A
(5)   B   D
(6)   B
(7)   D
(8) Selection line.

These eight classes thus receive a representative of each S chromosome through the father, and from the mother a variable number of S chromosomes or tester chromosomes T (A, B, D). Thus, each of the major chromosomes are heterozygous or homozygous for an S chromosome (in females). The eight classes make up all possible combinations between T chromosomes. By using females, the individual effects of the chromosomes and their interactions can be studied for a quantitative trait, whether it be chaeta number or a behavioural trait such as geotaxis. Furthermore, since there is no crossing over in the male in *Drosophila*, whole chromosomes may be maintained indefinitely by backcrossing males heterozygous for the S chromosomes and for a recessive marker on each chromosome, to females homozygous for the same recessive markers. One limitation of the technique is that it is only fully efficient in detecting recessive genes in the S chromosomes, since the comparison for each chromosome is between the heterozygote T/S and the homozygote

S/S. Genes in the selected chromosome S, dominant to their corresponding allele in the T chromosome will not be detected, and genes partially dominant will be detected with a variable degree of efficiency, according to the degree of dominance. Erlenmeyer-Kimling (see Hirsch, 1962) showed that the response to selection for positive geotaxis was due to factors on the X chromosome, and the response for negative geotaxis was due to factors on chromosome III. The unselected stock had factors for positive geotaxis on chromosome II. The effects of these factors were strengthened by selection for positive geotaxis and weakened by selection for negative geotaxis. Thus the analysis taken this far shows that there are genes distributed on the three major chromosomes of *Drosophila* influencing the response to gravity.

Similar experiments on geotaxis with the same type of apparatus have been carried out by Dobzhansky and Spassky (1962) in *D. pseudoobscura*. Selection in both positive and negative directions was effective in populations monomorphic as well as polymorphic for the third chromosome arrangements AR and CH. In polymorphic populations, it was found that selection for positive geotaxis favoured the carriers of AR chromosomes, while that for negative geotaxis gave an advantage to the AR/CH heterokaryotypes. Relaxation of selection led to a partial relapse towards the original state, indicating that the gene pool had not been made homozygous for geotactic response. Thus using selection techniques, an association between the third chromosome karyotypes and the behavioural trait geotaxis has been found in *D. pseudoobscura*. It is worth here recalling the associations of karyotype with mating speed and duration of copulation discussed in Chapters Two and Three.

In both of these experiments on geotaxis, some of the response to selection has been localized to specific chromosomes. In mammals these techniques are generally not available, or require a very lengthy breeding programme. However, theoretically it is possible to take this type of analysis substantially farther, and to localize regions of chromosomes and even loci controlling a response to selection, as will be seen later in this chapter.

In *D. robusta*, Carson (1958) selected for motility from one bottle to another towards a light source under strictly controlled environmental conditions. He was thus selecting for a trait which is a combination of phototaxis and motility. This trait has the advantage of allowing the testing of a large number of individuals extremely rapidly. Selection was carried out on ten strains homozygous for structural arrangements, and fifteen strains heterozygous for structural arrangements. Only positive selection lines were set up. Over a period of six generations the average response to selection was greater in the lines homozygous than in the lines heterozygous for rearrangements. It was suggested by Carson that this is related to the greater amount of free recombination which occurs in the structurally homozygous lines. In the structurally heterozygous lines, blocks of polygenes are tied together as gene complexes by inversion heterozygosity, which thus prevents extensive repatterning of the genotype by recombination, and hence the ultimate response to selection was restricted.

In *D. melanogaster* Manning (1961) selected for fast and slow mating speeds based on fifty pairs of virgin flies, aged four to six days, mated together in a mating chamber. The ten fastest and ten slowest pairs were taken to initiate fast and slow selection lines. Two fast and two slow lines were formed and a control line was maintained during part of the experiment. The response to selection was almost immediate, as would be predicted from the heritabilities for mating speed given in Section 3.6. After twenty-five generations the mean mating speed was of the order of three minutes in the fast lines, and eighty minutes in the slow lines. The divergence between the lines at generation 18 is shown in Fig. 4.6. Considerable variations in speed due to environmental fluctuations occurred during selection, but the fluctuations were generally similar in all lines for a given generation. Little genetic analysis was carried out on the selection lines except that an approximate heritability of 0·30 was computed from the rate at which the selection lines diverged during the first few generations.

Manning (1961), however, analysed the behavioural consequences of selection in some detail. Hybridizing the fast and slow lines in both directions gave intermediate F_1 mating speeds, while by intercrossing the two fast and two slow lines themselves in both directions gave fast and slow speeds respectively. These results indicate that both sexes were affected by selection. Confirmation of this came from testing mating speeds against an unselected stock of flies, when both sexes of the selected lines gave altered mating speeds in the expected directions.

Activity differences between lines were measured by admitting flies to an arena where the number of squares entered by a fly in a given time period was scored. The slow lines exhibited much more

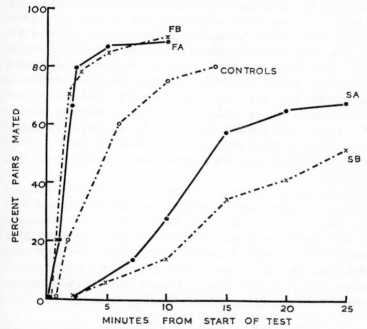

FIG. 4.6 Graphs of mating speeds for two lines selected for fast speeds (FA, FB), two for slow speeds (SA, SB), and controls, at the eighteenth generation of selection. (After Manning, 1961.)

activity of this type, which Manning called 'general activity' than the fast lines. Experiments using unselected females with selected males showed that the lag before courtship was much smaller for the fast than the slow lines; similarly, the frequency of licking was higher in the fast than in the slow lines. Thus, the fast lines have a high level of 'sexual activity' and a low level of 'general activity', and the slow lines a low level of 'sexual activity' and a high level of 'general activity'. Under natural conditions, these two components are presumably at an optimum as over-responsiveness in either direction would be undesirable.

A difficulty for this trait is that selection operates on both sexes and there could be rather different genes controlling the response in the two sexes. Manning (1963) attempted to look into this further by selecting for mating speed based on the behaviour of one sex only. There was no response to selection for fast-mating males or slow-mating females, and a fast-mating female line was not set up. There was, however, a response in male lines selected for slow mating. In these lines, the mating speed of females was unaffected in early generations, but in later generations there was some reduction in mating speed. Behaviourally it was found that both sexes showed lower 'general activity' and the males reduced courtship activity. Manning was not, however, able to come to any definite conclusions concerning possible differences between sexes in the genetic control of mating behaviour. Clearly, further work is needed along these lines.

Finally, since in Section 3.3, the duration of copulation was shown to be partly under genetic control, selection lines for long and short durations have been set up in *D. melanogaster* (MacBean and Parsons, unpublished), giving responses in both directions. After selection the duration of copulation was found to be determined almost entirely by the genotype of the male as found in other experiments, both in *D. melanogaster* (Hosgood, MacBean, and Parsons, unpublished) and *D. pseudoobscura* (Sections 2.4 and 3.6.).

4.4 *Further possibilities for genetic analysis*

In some of the *Drosophila* experiments, especially those on geotaxis, some progress towards an understanding of the genetic control of the trait under selection was obtained by using methods which permitted genetic activity to be assigned to specific chromosomes. This is a step farther in the understanding of the genetic architecture of a trait, than the demonstration of additive and dominance variances controlling a trait as was discussed in the previous chapter. Although genetic activity for geotaxis was localized to specific chromosomes, it may be possible to locate the actual regions of the chromosomes controlling genetic activity, using further breeding techniques. Thoday (1961) and his colleagues have developed the techniques for this work to the level of finding specific loci responsible for the response to selection for sternopleural chaeta number in *D. melanogaster*. That is, they have managed to 'locate the polygenes' controlling a quantitative trait. This is clearly much more informative than the computation of variance components.

In attempting to isolate the genes controlling a quantitative trait, the first step is to locate genetic activity to specific chromosomes as described for geotaxis. The next step is to attempt to specify the actual regions of the chromosome with genetic activity. If a multiply marked chromosome is available, female flies heterozygous for the selection line and the marked chromosome can be backcrossed to the homozygous marked male, to provide information on the polygenic activity of different parts of the same chromosome by assaying the various recombinant classes for the trait under analysis. Mather (1942) was able to localize polygenic activity controlling abdominal chaeta number to specific regions of chromosomes in *D. melanogaster* by this technique. Thoday (1961) and his colleagues have arrived at a more specific location of polygenic differences which have been built up in selection experiments for sternopleural chaeta number in *D. melanogaster* by progeny testing the recombinants in the above cross, to determine the number of chaeta number classes that can be distinguished for each recombinant marker chromosome. The discussion which follows will be in terms of sternopleural chaeta numbers, but in theory any quantitative trait can be analysed in a similar way. Suppose a certain whole chromosome, determined by the technique already outlined, gives a higher value for chaeta number than that of a homologous chromosome marked with the recessive markers *a* and *b*. Females heterozygous for the marked chromosome *ab* and the chromosome with the high value are then backcrossed to a homozygous *ab/ab* stock. In the progeny, equal numbers of AB/*ab*, *ab*/*ab*, *a*B/*ab*, and A*b*/*ab* genotypes are assayed for chaeta number. (A and B are the dominant alleles of *a* and *b* respectively.)

Suppose that the 'high' effect is associated with an allele, H. The corresponding allele in the *ab* stock will then be a 'low' allele, L.

F

Initially only one such HL locus is assumed. Individuals heterozygous for the *ab* chromosome and the chromosome with the 'high' effect will be HAB/L*ab*, ABH/*ab*L, or AHB/*aL b*, according to the position of the HL locus in relation to the loci *a* and *b*. On the assumption that the HL locus is close enough to *a* and *b* for linkage to be detected, the first arrangement, HAB/L*ab*, will give results for chaeta number such that the recombinant class, L*a*B, will be similar to the parental class, L*ab*, while the other recombinant class, H*Ab*, will be similar to the other parental class, HAB. Analogous results will occur for ABH/*ab*L. However, the results from AHB/*aL b* will be more complicated. Double crossing-over can be ignored, since once the analysis has proceeded to this order of refinement, the marker loci *a* and *b* will usually be fairly close together. The AB class will be all H and the *ab* class all L. A proportion of the recombinant A*b* class will be H and the rest L, according to whether recombination occurs between the HL locus and the *b* locus, or between the *a* locus and the HL locus. Similarly, from the reciprocal recombinant class *a*B, a proportion of recombinants will be H and a proportion L. The parental classes will then have distinct means but low variances as they are homogeneous; however, the recombinant classes will have higher variances as they are heterogeneous, but their means will be intermediate between the parental classes.

Suppose now that there are two chaeta-determining loci in coupling and both between the loci *a* and *b*. Then the heterozygotes prior to backcrossing will be AHHB/*a*LL*b*, and the homozygous marker stock *a*LL*b*/*a*LL*b*. Ignoring double crossing-over, the parental classes will be AHHB and *a*LL*b*, so that their means will differ and their variances will be low. The recombinant class A*b* will be AHH*b*, AHL*b*, or ALL*b* according to the position of the recombinational event. The recombinant class *a*B will similarly be *a*HHB, *a*LHB or *a*LLB. As before, the recombinant classes are heterogeneous with intermediate means and high variances. With one chaeta locus between the marker genes, each recombinant class, A*b* and *a*B, will have two categories, H and L. With two chaeta loci, each recombinant class will have three categories, and if there are *n* loci, each recombinant class will have *n* + 1 categories.

The next step is to progeny test some individuals from each of the recombinant classes A*b* and *a*B by crossing again to the homozygous marker stock *ab*/*ab* and scoring a number of offspring for chaeta number. If sufficient individuals are tested, it should be possible to determine how many categories occur in each of the classes A*b* and *a*B. From each progeny test, adequate individuals should be scored to place the individual under test into its appropriate category with a minimum possibility of misclassification. We should then be able to determine whether one, two, or more loci are involved. Naturally, the results will give a minimum number of loci, as some may be too small in effect to be detected. Based on the relative frequencies of progeny tested individuals falling into each category, estimates of recombination fractions can be made and a genetic map constructed.

The novel feature of Thoday's (1961) scheme is the progeny testing of individuals carrying the recombinant chromosomes. In complex situations progeny testing may take a few generations. In this way, polygenes can be located and mapped in the same way as if they were major genes. Thus, Thoday's work has improved the resolution of genetic analysis considerably, but further improvement of resolution may locate additional genes.

Thoday (1961) and his colleagues have found several discrete sternopleural chaeta loci on chromosomes II and III, using these techniques (Fig. 4.7). Thus in one selection line two chaeta loci at about 28 and 32 centi-Morgans (cMs) on the third chromosome were found, and several other loci have been found in other selection lines. Although only seven loci are given in Fig. 4.7, Thoday, Gibson, and Spickett (1963) have reported the location of thirteen loci influencing sternopleural chaeta number, one influencing fly size and one influencing both.

Two of these loci, which are at 27 and 47 cMs on the second chromosome are of particular interest. These loci were isolated by means of experimental disruptive (diversifying) selection, which usually involves choosing the two extreme classes of individuals for chaeta number to provide the parents of each generation. If $+$ represents more and $-$ fewer chaetae for these two loci, homozygotes $--/--$ were found to be lethal as were all individuals carrying the $++$ chromosome. This is a remarkable position effect extending over twenty map units, since $+-/-+$ is viable and $++/--$ is lethal.

The mechanism by which this could occur is obscure (Gibson and Thoday, 1962), especially as the map distance between the loci is far greater than has usually been found for position effects.

The discovery of this remarkable interacting pair of 'polygenes' amply justifies attempts to locate and study loci causing the responses to various forms of selection. Presumably the +— and —+ chromosomes were segregating in the stocks from which the experiments were set up. The wild stock, collected near Sheffield, England,

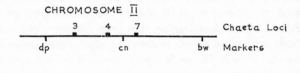

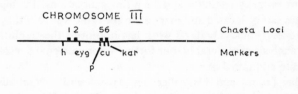

FIG. 4.7 The approximate location of chaeta loci, 1–7, found by Thoday and his colleagues. The genes used in locating the loci are also given. (After Thoday, 1961.)

which provided the material for the experiment, was tested. O forty-eight chromosomes assayed, forty-six were +— and two were —+, so that the base population was polymorphic.

Based on the same disruptive selection experiment, Wolstenholme and Thoday (1963) analysed two loci 2 cMs apart on the third chromosome at 49 and 51 cMs and found no evidence for interaction or lethality in contrast with the above results.

Taking into account all of Thoday's work, it is clear that sterno-pleural chaeta number is controlled by a very complex system of interacting genes occupying many positions in the genome. The genetic architecture of many other quantitative traits is likely to be equally or more complex, although evidence on other traits is sparse, however, Milkman (1962) has found polygenes for cross-veinless phenocopies.

The conclusion to be drawn from Thoday's work is that given adequately refined techniques, the genetic activity controlling quantitative traits can be localized and mapped at specific genetic loci. The continuous nature of the variation controlled by polygenes has in the past led naturally to the biometrical approach described in the previous chapter. This approach, being based on the analysis of variance of continuously varying traits, has led to the attitude that the underlying discontinuous variation, implicit in all segregation, is impossible to detect. However, as we have seen, there is no *a priori* reason to regard polygenes as different from major genes, so it seems reasonable to attempt to devise techniques as described above, so that the effects of polygenes can be amplified to the extent that they behave as major genes, and can be manipulated as major genes. In this case statistical and breeding techniques are used, but in other cases a refinement of biochemical techniques might be appropriate.

If we can locate 'polygenes', it becomes possible to study their direct effects and interactions with other similarly located 'polygenes', both for the trait under study and for fitness in general. It seems very important to attempt to locate 'polygenes' for a number of traits to see to what extent the assumptions made in biometrical genetics are realistic. These assumptions, which vary according to the exact model, are probably not critical when obtaining a general idea of the extent to which a trait is controlled by the genotype, but it seems difficult to say much more from routine biometrical experiments, especially when it is realized that different interpretations may be obtained if the scale is changed. In selection experiments, measures of heritability are only realistic in the stages of selection before the production of recombinants which may lead to accelerated responses. The nature of variability produced by recombination cannot be predicted by the heritability. Thus, the results of selection experiments enable us to appreciate some of the limitations of the methods presented in Chapter Three.

Since many behavioural traits are quantitative and may have quite high heritabilities, there is no *a priori* reason why the techniques of Mather and Thoday cannot be applied extensively to them. Perhaps the main difficulty is the likelihood of greater variation due to the environment than is found for the morphological traits more classically studied in this type of experiment.

Hence, a great deal of care must be taken to control environmental factors, as has been emphasized throughout. With regard to certain sexual traits such as mating speed, a further complication is that the quantitative values obtained depend to a greater or lesser extent on the interaction between two sexes. Furthermore, there may well be rather different genetic architectures involved in the two sexes, which would make the analysis extremely complex.

CHAPTER FIVE

The Evolutionary Consequences of Variations in Mating Behaviour

5.1 *Introduction*

In the last three chapters it has been shown that many behavioural traits are partly under genetic control. In this chapter the evolutionary consequences of variations in behavioural traits associated with mating will be discussed. Broadly speaking, we shall be concerned with any restriction or modification of random mating having a behavioural origin either within or between species.

The term *isolating mechanism* was proposed by Dobzhansky (1937) as a name for barriers to gene exchange between sexually reproducing populations. It is apt to give Mayr's (1963, p. 91) definition 'isolating mechanisms are biological properties of individuals that prevent the interbreeding of populations that are actually or potentially sympatric'. Sympatric populations are those occurring in the same locality, so that the definition excludes geographic isolation. One of the major mechanisms preventing gene exchange between species, or even between certain populations within species, is ethological isolation. Ethological isolating mechanisms are barriers to random mating due to incompatibilities in behaviour. To put ethological isolation into its proper context, a classification of isolating mechanisms essentially following Mayr (1963) is given below. They can be split into two major groups, namely mechanisms that prevent crosses (pre-mating mechanisms), and mechanisms that reduce the success of crosses even if there is mating (post-mating mechanisms).

Mayr purposely avoided the terms 'genetic' and 'physiological' in the classification, since genetic and physiological factors play a role in all the subdivisions.

Three important pre-mating mechanisms are (see also Ehrman' 1964 *a*):

(1) Potential mates do not meet (seasonal and habitat isolation).

(2) Potential mates meet but do not mate (ethological isolation).

(3) Copulation attempted but no transfer of gametes takes place (mechanical isolation).

Four important post-mating mechanisms are:

(1) Gametes transferred, but no fertilization occurs, so zygotes are not formed (gamete mortality).

(2) Death of zygotes occurs (hybrid inviability).

(3) The F_1 zygotes are viable, but are partly or completely sterile (hybrid sterility).

(4) The F_1 hybrids are fertile, but the fitness of the F_2 or back-cross hybrid is reduced (hybrid breakdown).

General discussions of isolating mechanisms have been given by many authors, notably Dobzhansky (1937, 1951) and Mayr (1963). The pre-mating mechanisms prevent wastage of gametes and so are highly susceptible to improvement by natural selection, while the post-mating mechanisms do not prevent gamete wastage, so their improvement by natural selection is difficult and indirect (Mayr, 1963). For the purposes of this discussion, we are concentrating on ethological isolating mechanisms, in particular those relating to mating, which probably constitute the largest and the most important class of isolating mechanisms (Mayr, 1963). Within species appropriate stimuli are exchanged between males and females which ultimately ensure mating, but between species the female may be non-receptive and ultimately the male breaks off his courtship. As discussed in Chapter Two, differing degrees of success for various genotypes may also occur within species, which could lead to non-random mating. Before discussing actual experimental data it is, however, necessary to briefly indicate some of the methods that have been used to assess variations between genotypes for mating success.

5.2 *Experimental approach*

In the previous chapters, when considering traits concerned with sexual behaviour such as mating speed and duration of copulation, single pair matings were usually considered, so permitting no choice for different genotypes within sexes. Even in experiments where several flies were placed in a mating chamber, members of a given sex were usually of the same type. However, in the study of deviations from random mating, experiments in which given males or females are allowed to choose between two or more distinct types of flies of the opposite sex must in general be carried out. Some of the experimental designs that have been used follow, but there are many variations of those presented:

(1) Two experiments consisting of females of types 1 and 2, with males of type 1 in one experiment, and type 2 in the other thus:

$$(1 + 2) \, ♀♀ \times 1 \, ♂♂$$
$$(1 + 2) \, ♀♀ \times 2 \, ♂♂.$$

This is a 'male choice' experiment since the males can choose one of two types of females, although naturally the female type may be relevant in the choice, perhaps by differing in levels of receptivity to the males.

(2) Two experiments consisting of males of types 1 and 2, with females of type 1 in one experiment, and type 2 in the other thus:

$$1 \, ♀♀ \times (1 + 2) \, ♂♂$$
$$2 \, ♀♀ \times (1 + 2) \, ♂♂.$$

This is a 'female choice' experiment, since the female can choose one of two males, although naturally the male type may be relevant in the choice; for example, by competing with each other for females.

(3) An experiment where females and males of two types 1 and 2 are put together thus:

$$(1 + 2) \, ♀♀ \times (1 + 2) \, ♂♂,$$

which is a situation perhaps most closely corresponding to natural conditions, and may be called a 'multiple choice' experiment.

(4) Separate or single pair matings as described in previous chapters thus: $1 ♀ × 1 ♂$, $2 ♀ × 2 ♂$, $1 ♀ × 2 ♂$, and $2 ♀ × 1 ♂$. If there is a higher frequency of matings in a given time for the first two mating types (homogamic matings), then isolation would be inferred. This approach is most successfully used for fairly distinct races between which there is a fairly strong tendency towards homogamic matings.

As well as different experimental designs, there are various methods of scoring, for example, by direct observation of the matings, or by dissection or progeny tests of females to look for evidence of sperm transfer.

In many cases, whatever the method of scoring, it is necessary to mark certain types. Several methods have been used, such as clipping the distal margins of the wings, marking with plastic colour dissolved in acetone, and dusting flies with a mixture of dye powder plus wheat flour. The critical point to ascertain is that the marking procedure does not affect mating. This can be verified by carrying out a control experiment.

With these comments we can look once again at the various experimental designs.

The first design presents no difficulties, since direct observation, or dissection or progeny tests of the females enables a classification. Multiple matings are likely for this design, and if the sequence for a given male is desired, direct observation is necessary, although to obtain this information the mating chamber must have very few males so that they can be followed individually. An appropriate mating chamber is described for the third design.

The second design is simple if direct observation is possible. If not, scoring must be done by progeny testing which in many situations may not reveal the identity of the male, especially when testing closely related races from natural populations.

The third design is essentially one for direct observation in a mating chamber, since otherwise progeny testing of females would be necessary. Direct observation has been facilitated by a mating chamber (Fig. 5.1) designed by Elens and Wattiaux (1964). The mating chamber is essentially a glass and wood sandwich. In the

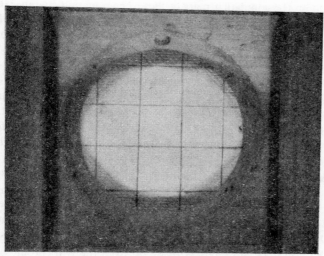

FIG. 5.1 Two views of the Elens–Wattiaux chamber, which is used for the direct observation of mating behaviour. A description is given in the text. (The photographs are from Ehrman, 1965.)

middle of the piece of wood a circle is cut out to form the mating chamber. The bottom of the chamber is formed by a chequered canvas. Through the small lateral hole in the wood, a number of flies are introduced without anaesthesia. Any marking of flies will have been done at least a day previously to avoid effects due to previous anaesthesia. Quite a large number of flies can be introduced, say up to sixty or more virgin pairs, but this will depend on the species. Copulating pairs do not generally move and so can be localized on the chequered canvas. This technique permits not only the observation of the types of males and females in a mating, but also the time at which it takes place, its sequence among other matings, and the duration of copulation. It does not permit the successive recording of matings of given single males unless very few flies are used. Certain other designs for mating chambers have been devised. If a large number of flies are to be studied, and measurements are required on the copulating pairs of flies, then a mating chamber large enough for mating pairs to be extracted with an aspirator is necessary, but multiple matings for a given fly are then not possible.

The scoring procedure for the fourth experimental design is by direct observation of mating speeds as described in previous chapters, or if mating tends to be slow as is likely if the strains are suspected of being rather distinct ethologically, female dissection or looking for evidence of progeny may be necessary.

Historically, the first design has been used extensively with dissection tests, but as will be seen in the next section, to make comparisons between experiments the overall percentage insemination in each experiment must be similar. Recently, however, the direct observation methods as described for the third design are being used more widely.

Many modifications of the techniques outlined are possible, e.g. in *D. pseudoobscura* we may be interested in the three karyotypes ST/ST, ST/CH and CH/CH made up from the two chromosomal arrangements ST and CH. Thus, more complex choice experiments involving all three karyotypes are possible.

Attention to environmental factors is critical, for example, *D. melanogaster* and *D. persimilis* show positive and *D. pseudoobscura* shows negative phototaxis (Pittendrigh, 1958). Thus in *D. pseudoob-*

scura strong illumination leads to movement ceasing after a few minutes in the chamber (Spiess and Langer, 1964 *a*). Furthermore, responses to light vary according to other environmental factors such as temperature or water balance (Pittendrigh, 1958). Thus the numerous environmental factors affecting mating behaviour, coupled with the series of different techniques which can be used, present a major difficulty when comparing experiments carried out by different workers. At the moment it is desirable to present an exact description of techniques in published work so that differences between experimenters are made obvious.

5.3 *Measures of sexual isolation*

The experimental designs given will provide an estimate of the degree of sexual isolation. We will use the term sexual isolation rather than ethological isolation in most of this chapter, since the experimental designs directly assess the results of courtship. Ethological isolation naturally includes sexual isolation, but has a wider meaning especially when considering the process of mating in the wild. For an estimate of sexual isolation, the relative proportions of homogamic and heterogamic matings, as discussed in the previous section, are necessary. For the male choice situation (design 1 above), let there be n_1 females of type 1 and n_2 of type 2, together with males of type 1. Further, let $x_{1,1}$ and $x_{1,2}$ be the numbers of type 1 and 2 females inseminated respectively, and let $p_{1,1} = \dfrac{x_{1,1}}{n_1}$ and $p_{1,2} = \dfrac{x_{1,2}}{n_2}$.

Stalker (1942) introduced an *isolation index*

$$b_{1,2} = \frac{p_{1,1} - p_{1,2}}{p_{1,1} + p_{1,2}} \tag{5.1}$$

The index can range from $+1$ for 100% homogamic matings to -1 for 100% heterogamic matings. When the index is zero there is no isolation. To see if deviations from $b_{1,2} = 0$ are significant, simple χ^2 tests can be carried out on the raw data for an expectation of $p_{1,1} = p_{1,2}$.

If the male is of type 2 and the two types of females are as before, a reciprocal isolation index

$$b_{2,1} = \frac{p_{2,2} - p_{2,1}}{p_{2,2} + p_{2,1}} \tag{5.2}$$

can be calculated, where $p_{2,2}$ and $p_{2,1}$ are defined in an analogous way to $p_{1,1}$ and $p_{1,2}$.

These indices depend on the overall proportion of females inseminated, i.e. on the duration of the experiment, so that for comparisons of indices from different experiments there should be a similar overall proportion inseminated. For this reason a number of experimenters terminate their experiments, so far as is possible, when about 50% of females have been inseminated (for example, Ehrman, 1964 b).

Levene (1949) proposed a *coefficient of isolation* which he showed to be less dependent on the proportion of females inseminated:

$$K_{1,2} = \frac{\log q_{1,1} - \log q_{1,2}}{\log q_{1,1} + \log q_{1,2}} \qquad (5.3)$$

where $q_{1,1} = 1 - p_{1,1}$ and $q_{1,2} = 1 - p_{1,2}$.

This is for males of strain 1 with females of both strains. The reciprocal coefficient of isolation using strain 2 males is

$$K_{2,1} = \frac{\log q_{2,2} - \log q_{2,1}}{\log q_{2,2} + \log q_{2,1}} \qquad (5.4)$$

where $q_{2,2} = 1 - p_{2,2}$ and $q_{2,1} = 1 - p_{2,1}$.

These coefficients have the same limiting values as $b_{1,2}$ and $b_{2,1}$.

Joint isolation indices based on the combination of the pairs of experiments with males of types 1 and 2 respectively have been proposed. If there are equal numbers of females or couples of each of the two types, the *joint isolation index* comes to

$$\frac{x_{1,1} + x_{2,2} - x_{1,2} - x_{2,1}}{N} \qquad (5.5)$$

where $N = x_{1,1} + x_{2,2} + x_{1,2} + x_{2,1}$, the total number of matings (Malogolowkin-Cohen *et al.*, 1965). If there are not equal numbers of females or couples the arithmetic mean of the two indices $b_{1,2}$ and $b_{2,1}$ thus:

$$b_{1 \text{ and } 2} = \frac{b_{1,2} + b_{2,1}}{2} \qquad (5.6)$$

is used, and there is an analogous expression based on (5.3) and (5.4).

Indices analogous to (5.1)–(5.5) can, of course, be calculated from data collected according to design 2, the female choice experiments. Naturally from a multiple choice experiment (design 3), all the indices described so far can be computed, although the biological situation in the multiple choice experiment is different from that in designs 1 and 2. Index (5.5) is particularly suitable for multiple choice experiments.

If there is a general excess of homogamic matings over heterogamic matings, this is indicative of a degree of sexual isolation between the two types of individuals. Within a population or species, the term *positive assortative mating* is used to refer to a situation where there is a general tendency for like phenotypes to mate. Conversely, the term negative assortative mating is used to refer to a situation where there is a general tendency for unlike phenotypes to mate. There will be further discussions on positive assortative mating later in this chapter. The two terms, positive assortative mating and sexual isolation, are in a sense synonymous, although the term sexual isolation is used much more widely and is usual when discussing mating behaviour between races and species, whereas positive assortative mating is usually (but not always) restricted to phenomena within a given population.

One further index has been proposed (Bateman, 1949) which measures the relative mating propensity of females and is defined as

$$a_{1, 2} = \frac{b_{1, 2} - b_{2, 1}}{2} g \qquad (5.7)$$

which is positive if there is an excess of matings of females of type 1, and negative if there is an excess of matings of females of type 2 in a male choice experiment. There is an analogous index based on (5.3) and (5.4). This index really measures differences in sexual vigour of the two types of females, and so is an estimate of sexual selection which is defined by Darwin as the advantage certain individuals have over others of the same sex and species solely in respect to reproduction. An analogous index can be computed from female choice experiments for assessing differences in the sexual vigour of males.

Various indices have been proposed by other authors. Thus in *D. melanogaster*, where the males are often relatively indifferent to the genotype of the females, a simple index has been used by Petit (1958) in multiple choice experiments. If A is the number of females inseminated by males of type 1 say, of which there are a number a in the population, and if B is the number of females inseminated by males of type 2 say, of which there are a number b in the population, then a *coefficient of sexual selection* is:

$$K = \frac{A/a}{B/b} = \frac{A}{B} \cdot \frac{b}{a}, \qquad (5.8)$$

which goes to infinity if males of type 1 are preferred, and to zero if males of type 2 are preferred.

Most of the indices presented have been given standard errors in the original papers so that their significance can be assessed. However, provided equal numbers of each sex are used, equal numbers of homogamic and heterogamic matings will be expected in the isolation indices and coefficients if mating is at random, which can be tested with simple χ^2 tests. Even in more complex situations, observed data can be compared with what is expected assuming random mating, and the deviation from this expectation tested, using χ^2 tests. In the case of coefficients measuring differences in the sexual vigour of two types of males or females, the expectations will be based on the proportions of the two types in the population initially.

5.4 *Single genes and sexual isolation*

Early data based on direct observation, using female and male choice experiments were presented by Sturtevant (1915) for four mutant strains and a wild type strain in *D. melanogaster*. Thus for matings between white-eyed and wild-type flies, he obtained results as in Table 5.1. In the male choice experiment, the joint isolation index (equation 5.6) came to 0.097, and in the female choice experiment to 0.026. Thus there is little evidence for choice of mates leading to isolation, as these values are close to zero. However, the relative mating propensity (equation 5.7) of wild-type females compared with white came to −0·303 in the male choice experiments, while the relative mating propensity of wild type males compared with white in the female choice experiments came to 0·558, thus there is some evidence for non-random mating due to differences in the vigour of sexual behaviour, i.e. there is sexual selection.

TABLE 5.1 Results from male and female choice experiments between white-eyed and wild-type *Drosophila melanogaster*
(After Sturtevant, 1915)

(a)	Male choice	Number of females mated	
	Wild-type male	Wild-type 54	White-eyed 82
	White-eyed male	Wild-type 40	White-eyed 93
(b)	Female choice	Number of males mated	
	Wild-type female	Wild-type 53	White-eyed 14
	White-eyed female	Wild-type 62	White-eyed 19

Merrell (1949) studied the effect on mating of four sex-linked mutations, singly and in combination in the same fly, using male and female choice experiments. By using females heterozygous for the mutant, for example, raspberry (*ras*), female choice experiments could be carried out by progeny testing. Thus for *ras* and + males mated with a *ras*/+ female, progeny are obtained as follows:

$$\frac{ras}{+} \female \times ras \male - \tfrac{1}{2}\frac{ras}{ras}\female : \tfrac{1}{2}\frac{ras}{+}\female$$

$$\tfrac{1}{2} ras \male : \tfrac{1}{2} + \male$$

$$\frac{ras}{+} \female \times + \male - \tfrac{1}{2}\frac{ras}{+}\female : \tfrac{1}{2}\frac{+}{+}\female$$

$$\tfrac{1}{2} ras \male : \tfrac{1}{2} + \male.$$

The presence of mutant female progeny indicates the success of the mutant male.

Deviations from random mating occurred more often and were greater in the female choice experiments. Thus wild-type males were much more successful than yellow (*y*) males (as expected – see Section 2.2), and were moderately more successful than cut (*ct*) and *ras* males, while forked (*f*) males were equivalent to the wild type in mating success. In combination, the effects of the mutant genes were

G

mainly additive but in some cases involving *ras*, the additivity broke down, in particular, *ct ras* males were superior to either *ct* or *ras* males. In the male choice experiments, deviations from random mating were most evident for the less vigorous males. Presumably the less vigorous male was rejected by the less receptive female so leading to deviaticns from random mating. In the case of vigorous males, the female's reaction to the male's courtship pattern is probably less important than for less vigorous males. The conclusion was that selective mating was important in these experiments, but there was no tendency for like phenotypes to mate leading to an excess of homogamic matings, indicating sexual isolation.

In subsequent experiments Merrell (1953) studied gene frequency changes in populations each containing one of the four sex-linked genes. Initially the populations had equal numbers of mutant and wild-type males and only heterozygous females, so that the gene frequency of the mutants was 0·5. In all cases the frequency of the mutant genes fell quite rapidly over a number of generations. The experimental results agreed with results predicted by taking into account the levels of selective mating for these mutants, consequently selective mating was a major factor in the decline in frequency of the mutant genes. This demonstrates the importance of selective mating as a component of fitness in the populations under study.

Petit (1958) has carried out fairly extensive multiple choice experiments. She showed that the influence of the genotype of the females was unimportant compared with that of the males in her experiments, and so proceeded to compute K, her coefficient of sexual selection (equation 5.8). Her calculations showed that Bar males were always disadvantageous compared with wild-type males. This disadvantage was most pronounced when Bar was most frequent. For white and wild-type males, the white males were disadvantageous when 40–80% of the males in the population were white, but outside these limits when white males were rare or abundant they were advantageous. Thus mating success depends on the proportion as well as the nature of competing genotypes. It will be recalled that evidence of this nature was presented for *D. pseudoobscura* in Section 2.4, where the rare type was advantageous in some cases. Further investigations of phenomena of this nature will be awaited with great interest. Petit's experiments also showed the influence of environmental variables such as temperature and food on mating success.

These various experiments with mutant genes show the existence of sexual selection determined by differences in the vigour of one or both sexes, although in general no assortative mating was found. There are a number of other experiments reported in the literature (for example, Rendel, 1951), but space does not permit their discussion here. From the evolutionary point of view, however, experiments with different genotypes or races occurring in the wild are of more importance and work of this type will now be discussed.

5.5 Mating success within and between strains

In this section we will briefly consider experiments on different strains within species of *Drosophila*. In *D. willistoni* slight mating preferences have been shown in male choice experiments between Brazilian and Guatemalan strains (Dobzhansky and Mayr, 1944), and in *D. prosaltans* striking differences were found between Brazilian, Guatemalan, and Mexican strains (Dobzhansky and Streisinger, 1944). In these two species most of the mating preferences are one-sided, as a greater proportion of females of one than of the other strain were inseminated by males of both strains, that is there is sexual selection rather than sexual isolation.

However, in *D. sturtevanti*, male choice experiments show two-sided mating preferences for homogamic matings, so that there is a tendency towards sexual isolation (Dobzhansky, 1944). The strains came from Tamazunchale in Mexico, Quiriguá in Guatemala, Belém in northern Brazil, Rio de Janeiro, and Bertioga in the state of São Paulo, Brazil. In all the possible crosses, a positive isolation index (calculated according to equations (5.1) and (5.2)) was obtained, showing that the males inseminate more females of their own strain than those of other strains. The highest indices came from the two geographically most remote localities (Tamazunchale, Mexico, and Bertioga, Brazil), although some localities nearly as remote (Tamazunchale and Rio de Janeiro) failed to show statistically significant isolation indices. Strains from geographically close localities either showed no isolation (Rio de Janeiro and Bertioga) or considerable isolation (Tamazunchale and Quiriguá), and strains showing no isolation from each other occasionally behaved very differently with respect to other strains.

However, in spite of the correlation with geographical isolation being far from clear, the strains of D. *sturtevanti* from different regions do show incipient sexual isolation because of the excess of homogamic matings. True sexual isolation of this type reduces gene exchange between the populations under investigation more than in the one-sided mating preferences of D. *willistoni* and D. *prosaltans*.

The hybrids between two strains each possessing a genotype well-adapted to its own environment are likely to be ill-balanced and unfit for survival. This will reduce the effective gene exchange between populations, so that a reduction of gene exchange may be favoured by natural selection. Any genetic variants reducing the rate of exchange will be favoured until a complete cessation of gene exchange is obtained. This may be aided by any form of isolating mechanism, including sexual isolation, which may evolve during divergence. Dobzhansky (1944) regards the one-sided mating preferences as found regularly for mutant genes and for populations within certain species, as by-products of physiological (and hence behavioural) differences. He considers that sexual isolation may develop from one-sided mating preferences by the co-ordinating action of natural selection.

D. *paulistorum* is a taxon which contains an extraordinary complex of geographic races or incipient species. Five have almost reached the status of reproductively isolated but morphologically indistinguishable species. They are the Centro-American, Orinocan, Amazonian, Andean – South Brazilian and Guianan races (Carmody et al., 1962). These are mainly but not always allopatric (i.e. occur in different geographic localities), and when placed together, females of one and males of another race exhibit pronounced and, in some cases, nearly complete sexual isolation. If hybrids are produced, the females are fertile and the males sterile. Thus there are two isolating mechanisms, sexual isolation and hybrid sterility. Sexual isolation is determined by polygenic differences between the races, while hybrid sterility involves a remarkable predetermination of the egg cytoplasm by the genotype present in the egg before meiosis and fertilization (Ehrman, 1960, 1961).

A sixth race, called the Transitional race, occurs in Colombia. All strains of this race can be crossed and will produce fertile hybrids with at least one of the other five races (Dobzhansky and Spassky, 1959). Because of the Transitional race, *D. paulistorum* can perhaps be regarded as a single species, although this is a matter of opinion. It therefore has a single but extremely dissected and differentiated gene pool, and represents a good example of a situation where it is difficult to decide whether there are one or several species.

Carmody *et al.* (1962) scored by female dissection tests, a series of sixty-seven male choice experiments where all flies belonged to the same race, but usually to strains of different geographic origin. About half of the isolation indices were significant at least at the 5% level, which suggests that random mating is by no means a general rule in intraracial crosses. Positive indices were more common than negative indices, so that even for geographic strains of the same race, homogamic matings are more frequent than heterogamic ones.

For interracial crosses positive isolation indices were quite general, although there are variations between races. It is noteworthy that the Transitional race is transitional with regard to sexual isolation, since the average isolation index in crosses of other races with the Transitional race is +0·65, and +0·87 in crosses between other races (Table 5.2).

One final observation (Ehrman, 1965) of interest is based on the multiple choice method using the Elens–Wattiaux (Fig. 5.1) mating chambers and scoring by direct observation. Joint isolation coefficients (equation 5.5) were computed for given pairs of races which have been found to occur both sympatrically and allopatrically. In allopatric crosses the average isolation coefficient was 0·67, and in sympatric crosses 0·85. Thus pairs of races occurring sympatrically exhibit a greater degree of sexual isolation than the same pairs occurring allopatrically, or races coexisting geographically tend to be reproductively more isolated than those that do not, which is reasonable as the production of large numbers of hybrids would be very inefficient.

In conclusion, the species *D. paulistorum* makes up a biologically intriguing situation as it contains populations at all stages of sexual isolation ranging from apparent identity to almost complete separation. Furthermore, there is hybrid sterility as a further isolating mechanism.

TABLE 5.2   Mean isolation indices in crosses between different races of *D. paulistorum*

(After Carmody *et al.*, 1962)

Cross	Isolation index*
Transitional × Centro-American	+0·675
Transitional × Amazonian	+0·577
Transitional × Andean	+0·458
Transitional × Orinocan	+0·824
Transitional × Guianan	+0·775
Average with Transitional	+0·650
Amazonian × Andean	+0·945
Amazonian × Guianan	+0·860
Andean × Guianan	+0·895
Centro-American × Amazonian	+1·000
Centro-American × Andean	+0·777
Centro-American × Orinocan	+0·785
Centro-American × Guianan	+1·000
Orinocan × Amazonian	+0·883
Orinocan × Andean	+0·837
Orinocan × Guianan	+0·875
Average without Transitional	+0·874

* Means of indices (equation 5.1) derived from a series of male choice experiments. So far as possible all insemination frequencies were kept close to 50% so that indices from different experiments could be compared.

Many other papers could be cited on these and other species, however, the evidence quoted is adequate to show the general situation. Different populations or strains within a species may show sexual selection with respect to each other for physiological reasons. As we go closer to the dividing line between species, the greater the isolation index and the greater the degree of sexual isolation. Geographical isolation may, but not necessarily, lead to sexual isolation. Broadly speaking, there seems to be a correlation between geographical and sexual isolation, but there are numerous exceptions. We now discuss mating success between species, remembering that the races of *D. paulistorum* can be argued to be species.

5.6 *Mating success between species*

The expectation is for complete sexual isolation between species, that is, all matings would be expected to be homogamic. However, it is pertinent to comment briefly on the sexual behaviour of closely related species. In general (Spieth, 1958), closely related species of *Drosophila* have the same basic courtship and mating behaviour. The differences which apparently prevent the successful synchronization of the behaviour patterns of the two sexes in interspecific combinations are quantitative rather than qualitative. However, as species diverge phylogenetically as determined by various criteria such as structure, ecology, distribution, etc., the observable mating behaviour diverges more obviously. As Spieth (1958) points out, exceptions may occur to these rules, but they form reasonable generalizations.

Spieth (1958) mentions some pairs of species which appear to have qualitatively similar mating behaviour and live in the same area. That is, they are sympatric, and yet at the same time they maintain their identity and so represent separate species. We wish to know how these populations are isolated, and whether ethological isolating mechanisms are relevant. When such pairs of species are morphologically almost indistinguishable, they are referred to as sibling species.

The species *D. pseudoobscura* and *D. persimilis* represent such a pair of sibling species which are sympatric in some regions. In regions where the species are sympatric, isolation is maintained by several factors, some of which are:

(1) somewhat different habitat preferences such that *D. persimilis* occurs in cooler moister niches and *D. pseudoobscura* in warmer drier niches;

(2) some differences in food preferences;

(3) different diurnal periods of maximum activity; and

(4) sexual isolation.

The first three, which are ecological–physiological but obviously with behavioural components, are not entirely effective as both species have been found feeding side by side in the same slime flux on the black oak, *Quercus kellogii* (Carson, 1951), so that the absence of interspecific matings in natural habitats is perhaps largely due to ethological isolation (Dobzhansky, 1951). Furthermore, when interspecific matings take place in the laboratory, fewer sperm are transferred than in intraspecific crosses, the F_1 males are sterile, and the F_1 female progeny from backcrosses have reduced vigour.

In the laboratory, hybridization will occur relatively readily, but virgins were usually four days old when utilized. However, when flies of both sexes and species were placed together a few hours after emergence the proportion of hybrids was lower. Spieth (1958) considers that this higher level of isolation may be due to individuals of both species maturing together, and acquiring the ability to discriminate between species before becoming sexually mature. In further experiments, it was found that the *D. persimilis* female once having mated with a *D. persimilis* male, will not accept a *D. pseudoobscura* male subsequently.

Thus the high level of isolation found between these two species is due to ethological isolation enhanced by various other pre-mating isolating mechanisms as well as hybrid male sterility, a post-mating isolating mechanism. Under laboratory conditions, where conditions are different from those prevailing in the wild, the degree of isolation may be somewhat reduced. Finally, it seems likely that isolation in the wild may not only be innate but partially learned.

Sexual isolation has been studied between two further sibling species, *D. melanogaster* and *D. simulans* (Sturtevant, 1929; Barker, 1962). In general, it seems that ethological isolating mechanisms almost completely prevent matings, and that such hybrids that are formed are sterile. Where matings do occur under laboratory conditions, the genotype and age of the flies are important. In mass cultures more matings occur than when set up as single pairs, perhaps because of facilitation among courting males whereby one courtship stimulates the other males in the same culture to increased activity. Other genera are discussed by Spieth (1958).

More recently work has appeared on two South American sibling species, *D. gaucha* and *D. pavani* (Koref-Santibañez, 1964), which show little discrimination in courtship behaviour, and crosses yield abundant but sterile progenies. Thus the main isolating mechanism is hybrid sterility. In nature the lack of discrimination in courtship behaviour is unimportant, since except for a small part of Argentina where the two species are found together, they are allopatric. It may be expected that greater divergence in courtship behaviour would occur in sympatric rather than allopatric species (e.g. compare the evidence in the previous section for allopatric and sympatric pairs of races in *D. paulistorum*) so as to avoid the production of large numbers of relatively unfit hybrids.

5.7 *Modification and evolution of sexual isolation in laboratory populations*

In this section we will discuss experimental evidence showing that the degree of sexual isolation within and between species can be modified by direct and indirect selection. The section will be concluded by citing evidence for assortative mating within a population and discussing its possible evolutionary consequences.

Koopman (1950) set up artificial mixed populations of the two sibling species, *D. persimilis* and *D. pseudoobscura*, using marked stocks. Mating was carried out at 16° C because close to this temperature sexual isolation between the two species has been found to be relatively low (Mayr and Dobzhansky, 1945). Selection was carried out each generation for pure-bred flies, that is, the progeny of parents that had bred homogamically. Isolation developed rapidly after a few generations, and part of the reproductive isolation developed was shown by sexual isolation tests to be behavioural. The experiments also show that the level of sexual isolation depends on the environment, in this case temperature, and that even if isolation is reduced as was observed initially at 16° C, it can be built up again in a remarkably short amount of time, so reducing the proportion of hybrids to a low level. Koopman aided the change by removing the hybrids each generation, in this way simulating complete hybrid inviability.

In *D. melanogaster*, Wallace (1954) allowed straw and sepia virgin females and males to interbreed, and in subsequent generations kept the mutant flies and discarded the hybrids, so artificially selecting for homogamic matings. Tests during the seventy-third generation revealed a strong tendency for homogamic sepia matings. Similarly Knight, Robertson, and Waddington (1956) began with a population containing ebony and vestigial flies and discarded the hybrids each generation. After thirty to thirty-five generations the proportion of hybrids was reduced substantially, probably due to changes of female behaviour such that the females became less willing to crossbreed after selection.

Koref-Santibañez and Waddington (1958) searched for mating preferences between strains of *Drosophila melanogaster* that had been genetically isolated for many generations, using male and female choice experiments. In four of six inbred strains they found occasional preferences for homogamic matings in male choice experiments, and in two of the four the same tendency was found in female choice experiments. They argued that the tendency towards homogamic matings is initially a chance phenomenon, and so suggest that the initial steps towards sexual isolation may be sometimes attributable to chance. In a further eight strains, four of which had been selected for high, and four for low abdominal chaeta numbers, they found that mating was nearly at random. Mather and Harrison (1949), using the male choice method, found mating preferences between two inbred strains of *D. melanogaster*, and also between strains selected for abdominal chaeta number which were based on an initial cross between the two inbred strains. These experiments all show that sexual selection and isolation may arise in certain circumstances as a concomitant to genetic divergence.

In *D. pseudoobscura*, Ehrman (1964 *b*) studied sexual isolation between six populations set up in cages at the same time by M. Vetukhiv and derived from the same initial population. Of the populations, two were maintained at each of 16° C, 25° C and 27° C. After four years and five months male choice experiments of the type:

$$10 \text{ A } \male\male \times 10 \text{ A } \female\female + 10 \text{ B } \female\female$$
and
$$10 \text{ B } \male\male \times 10 \text{ A } \female\female + 10 \text{ B } \female\female$$

were carried out, where A and B represent flies from different cages. The choice experiments were carried out at 16° C and 27° C, the two extreme temperatures at which the populations were kept. The females of one population were marked by slightly clipping the wings for identification, and scoring was by female dissection tests. Ehrman calculated isolation indices (equations 5.1 and 5.2) which could be compared with each other since the percentage of females inseminated was close to 50% in all instances. In Table 5.3 joint isolation indices

TABLE 5.3   Joint isolation indices from six isolated populations
of D. pseudoobscura

(After Ehrman, 1964 b)

Populations crossed	° C	Index
A × B	16	+0·097
	27	+0·209
C × D	16	+0·090
	27	+0·190
E × F	16	+0·052
	27	+0·106
A × C	16	+0·075
	27	+0·014
A × E	16	+0·154
	27	+0·016
C × E	16	+0·011
	27	+0·105

Environments of populations:

A and B at 16° C
C and D at 25° C
E and F at 27° C

(equation 5.6) are presented between the six populations. It will be noted that sexual isolation is as pronounced within temperatures as between temperatures, so that sexual isolation evidently takes place between isolated populations kept in similar as well as in different environments. Sexual isolation has arisen in the absence of any selection for isolation and is evidently a by-product of genetic divergence. Thus geographical separation may facilitate the achievement of reproductive isolation, presumably because within each cage there was some reorganization of the gene pool during the period of isolation, such that each cage built up its own unique highly adapted gene complex, with its own behavioural phenotype.

Ehrman's results are of interest in relation to those of Gibson and Thoday (1962) who practised disruptive (diversifying) selection for high and low sternopleural chaeta numbers in *D. melanogaster* in a single population maintaining gene flow between the high and low components (see Section 4.4). Disruptive selection is the situation where the two extremes of a distribution of measurements for a quantitative trait are selected, and the intermediates in the distribution are selected against. As a result of selection, the population tended to split into two discrete sub-populations characterised by high and low chaeta numbers. This occurred within ten generations. Thus the population became bimodal and hence polymorphic under disruptive selection as was predicted by Mather (1955). This is a polymorphism in which the heterozygotes are disadvantageous, since under disruptive selection the extremes are favoured. Under random mating the heterozygote must be fitter than the two corresponding homozygotes for a balanced polymorphism to occur (see Section 2.3).

Maynard Smith (1962) has shown that a polymorphism in the absence of heterozygote advantage can be maintained under the specialized situation of the two extreme genotypes of the population being adapted to different ecological niches with gene flow between the niches, such that in niche 1 AA > Aa > aa in fitness and in niche 2 aa > Aa > AA. That is, the fitnesses are in the opposite sense in the two niches, and so is a situation formally equivalent to disruptive selection. This, with one or two further restrictions, has led Maynard Smith to argue that except under special circumstances, it is difficult to imagine disruptive selection leading to rapid isolation in the wild. Mayr (1963) has arrived at similar conclusions. Maynard Smith further considers on theoretical grounds that Gibson and Thoday's (1962) experimental results are very difficult to understand unless there is positive assortative mating for sternopleural chaeta number in the base population, or unless there is selection favouring positive assortative mating during the experiment, that is, there is selection favouring a greater proportion of flies with high chaeta numbers mating together and low chaeta numbers mating together, than would be expected under random mating.

Later results of Thoday (1964) have shown strong positive assortative mating within the high (H) and low (L) lines for tests carried out at various generations between the seventh and nineteenth of selection. In mating tests of the female choice type scored by progeny testing, there were

$$\left.\begin{array}{l} 71\ H\,\female \times H\,\male \\ 15\ H\,\female \times L\,\male \end{array}\right\} \quad \text{and} \quad \left.\begin{array}{l} 27\ L\,\female \times H\,\male \\ 62\ L\,\female \times L\,\male \end{array}\right\}$$

matings giving a joint isolation coefficient $b_{1\,\text{and}\,2}$ (equation 5.6) of 0·52. The change in mating behaviour clearly affected both sexes, so that the isolation developed by disruptive selection is associated with strong positive assortative mating within the sub-populations.

The question remains as to whether there is positive assortative mating for chaeta number in the base population prior to disruptive selection, or whether assortative mating arises *de novo* during selection. In the wild, positive assortative mating has not been commonly observed within populations, although it has been found between the various colour forms of the Blue Snow Goose (Cooch and Beardmore, 1959) and the Arctic Skua (O'Donald, 1959). The best evidence comes from man where positive assortative mating has been found for numerous traits such as stature and span (see Section 7.8). Assuming that these traits are heritable, then assortative mating must be, as Fisher (1930) argued, an agent important in modifying the genetic constitution of a population. Fisher (1930) concluded that the principal biometric effect of assortative mating is to increase the genetic variance of the population, and so increase the effect of selection on a trait.

In *D. melanogaster* the possibility of positive assortative mating for sternopleural chaeta number was tested (Parsons, 1965 *b*), by placing forty virgin females and males from an outbred Canton-S strain, aged three days, in a mating chamber. As soon as a pair commenced to mate it was sucked into a trap and then stored separately to await scoring for sternopleural chaeta number. Mating pairs were extracted until about one-half of the pairs had mated and then the remaining flies were stored together.

Correlation coefficients were computed between mated males and females for sternopleural chaeta number. For unmated flies correlation coefficients were calculated by arbitrarily pairing together flies as they were scored, so the coefficients obtained represent control values as pairing was approximately at random. For three different larval competition levels, the correlation coefficients obtained are presented in Table 5.4. For the mated pairs the coefficients are all

TABLE 5.4   Correlation coefficients (r) between members of pairs for sternopleural chaeta number in D. melanogaster

(After Parsons, 1965 b)

Larval competition level	Mated		Unmated	
	n	r	n	r
Low (twenty-five larvae per vial)	212	0·206*	247	−0·038
High (200 larvae per vial)	568	0·109*	610	−0·049
Mixed (a mixture of twenty adult males and females from Low and High)	172	0·200*	239	−0·005

* $P < 0·01$ — representing probability that r differs from 0.

significantly > 0, indicating positive assortative mating, and for those in the unmated category the coefficients are close to 0. Unpublished results give similar coefficients for abdominal chaeta number. These results could be a direct effect of fly size, as sternopleural chaeta number and fly size are directly correlated when fly size is altered by environmental means (Parsons, 1961), or perhaps there may be behavioural differences between flies of different sizes leading to minor modifications in courtship behaviour. For example, wing area which is probably related to fly size is a factor in determining male sexual success (Ewing, 1964). Thus there is positive assortative mating for sternopleural chaeta number in Drosophila populations, which may be accentuated by disruptive selection.

Such assortative mating for quantitative traits in Drosophila is based on one population. It is rather different from the sexual isolation found between strains and mutants discussed earlier in this chapter, since when considering strains and mutants we may be considering the possibility of sexual isolation between two populations, perhaps with differing gene pools. There is a great need to see to what extent assortative mating for quantitative traits occurs in natural populations, especially in those cases where it is possible to assess the degree to which the trait under investigation is controlled genetically.

5.8 Conclusions

In this chapter we have discussed two forms of non-random mating, namely sexual selection and sexual isolation. Sexual selection represents the reproductive advantage certain individuals have over others of the same sex, and is probably due to differences in physiological and behavioural vigour between individuals. It has been found mainly between mutant strains within species. Sexual isolation, however, is a general tendency towards homogamic matings, and so may lead to a tendency for gene pools to be isolated. Within populations, the term positive assortative mating is often used with a similar meaning. A tendency for homogamic matings is often found between geographically remote strains, especially in organisms such as *D. paulistorum*, which is a complex of races or species, according to one's point of view. Between species, homogamic matings are almost universal, although sometimes hybrids may be found but they are usually unfit and so are eliminated from the population.

The degree of sexual isolation is modifiable both in nature and in the laboratory, which is reasonable in view of its importance in maintaining intact the gene pools of various species. Of considerable interest in this respect will be future research on allopatric and sympatric races and species. The observation in *D. paulistorum* of more isolation between pairs of races when sympatric than when allopatric, shows the likely evolution of levels of sexual isolation in the wild. Conversely, the low level of sexual isolation between the sibling species *D. pavani* and *D. gaucha*, which are mainly allopatric, is reasonable as the species do not contact each other except in a very small region. In general then, sexual isolation between discrete gene pools can be developed by artificial or natural selection, although sexual isolation may develop fortuitously as a result of genetic divergence, as has been shown from comparisons of populations and strains within species which were set up for other purposes.

Positive assortative mating for quantitative traits within a given population in *Drosophila* also has been discussed. This will lead to genetic diversity. The fuller evaluation of the importance of assortative mating must, however, await further research, as must the importance of disruptive selection in the formation of new races and species.

Since the evidence cited is from *Drosophila*, care must be taken when attempting to extrapolate to other organisms, especially those in phylogenetically diverse groups. However, in a monograph of this nature where an attempt is being made to show how genetic components in behaviour can be analysed, it is felt that further discussions, which would be based mainly on observations in the wild, would make the text excessively long. In any case, a certain amount of further work will be discussed on behaviour in rodents and man in the next two chapters.

CHAPTER SIX

Genotype and Behaviour in Rodents

6.1 *Introduction*

Behaviour in rodents has been studied extensively. There are many reports of single genes affecting behaviour, and a number of studies of a more biometrical nature.

Single genes will be discussed very little. However, at a conference held in mid-1965, it was announced that there are ninety-two neurological mutants known in the mouse (Sidman, Appel, and Fuller, 1965), which were classified by D. S. Falconer into defects of regional development, structural defects of individual cells that fail to make some special product, and functional defects requiring biochemical study. Most of the known mutant disorders affect the nervous system during its development. Several, for example, affect the cerebellum. A number of mutations affect the inner ear and related structures, leading to a primary disorder in the early embryonic central nervous system, interfering with subsequent induction of peripheral structures. The detailed study of the biochemical, developmental, and behavioural consequences of these mutants will be helpful in the analysis of certain neurological diseases of man. Naturally mutants with a neurological effect are also known in other rodents.

Evidence for a degree of genetic control of many quantitative traits, especially in rats, mice, and guinea pigs has been found. In the next section of this chapter, the types of traits studied will be given with some conclusions, without attempting to be exhaustive. There will also be a brief discussion of sexual selection experiments (see Chapter Five). Good reviews providing more details are by Fuller and Thompson (1960) and Broadhurst (1960), and discussions of the application of biometrical genetics to behavioural traits are given by Broadhurst and Jinks (1961, 1963).

The next section will be followed by a discussion of certain behavioural traits having a biochemical as well as a genetic basis. The biochemical basis of behaviour has been rather more investigated in rodents than in *Drosophila*, and offers a fruitful field for research, especially if combined with genetics.

6.2 *Quantitative traits*

Quantitative behavioural traits where some degree of genetic control has been found, either from analyses of inbred strains, their hybridsl and perhaps other generations, or from selection experiments, will be mentioned here.

Activity level. This has been measured in rats and mice in various ways, and clear differences between strains have been found for most measures, such as running speeds in mazes of various designs (Fuller and Thompson, 1960), and the number of squares crossed on a floor in a given period of time (Broadhurst, 1960 – see Section 4.2; McClearn, 1961). McClearn's (1961) study, like Broadhurst's, was genetically more sophisticated than most as the F_1, F_2, B_1, and B_2 generations were bred from two parental inbred strains of mice, one showing high and one low activity. Heritabilities in the broad sense from 0·42 to 0·84 were obtained.

Activity has also been measured in activity wheels where revolutions are counted photoelectrically. Using this approach Bruell (1964 *a*) found differences between strains of mice. In many cases the hybrids showed greater activity than their parents, i.e. they showed behavioural heterosis as described in Section 3.6 for mating speed in *Drosophila*. In rats, Rundquist (1933) successfully selected for active and inactive strains based on activity in a revolving drum. Some genetical experiments were carried out by Brody (see Section 4.1) on these selection lines, from which she claimed the detection of a major gene with modifier genes controlling activity.

A number of experimenters have studied the inheritance of one rather special aspect of activity, namely exploration. It can be measured as the number of arms traversed by an animal in a simple T- or Y-maze, no incentive being offered other than the exploration itself. Another method is to use an open field, divided either by barriers or a grid on the floor into a number of sections. The number of sections traversed in a certain time period is used as a measure of exploration. Differences in exploratory activity have been found for some inbred strains of mice by using these various techniques (Fuller and Thompson, 1960). A more complete genetic analysis based on the two inbred strains showing extremes of high and low activity, and their F_1, F_2, and backcross generations, tested in an open field and a Y-maze showed activity to be controlled by genes with large additive effects (see Broadhurst and Jinks, 1961, for analysis). Fuller and Thompson (1960) cite other references. Bruell (1946 b) placed mice individually into a four-compartment maze. As a mouse moved from one compartment to another it interrupted a light beam which activated a photo-relay and counter. The exploration score of an animal consisted of the total count registered in ten minutes of testing. Differences between strains were found and their hybrids showed behavioural heterosis as for activity wheels.

Sexual behaviour. Goy and Jakway (1959) and Jakway (1959) studied sexual behaviour in the guinea pig in two inbred strains, and the F_1, F_2, B_1, and B_2 generations. For females the response to the injection of female hormone was assessed in terms of four behavioural measures elicited experimentally by tests for lordosis, which is the arching of the back prior to copulation. For the males, females in heat were used as the stimulus and six behavioural measures were taken. Broadhurst and Jinks (1963) found difficulties in scaling for all the variables except two, namely the number of male-like mountings during oestrous for females, and the number of penile intromissions for males. Estimates of heritability (in the narrow sense) fell between about 0·50 and 0·60 for these traits, and there was a marked dominance component for both traits. Heterosis was found for the highest measures of activity in males, namely the intromission rate and number of ejaculations. In mice between strain differences have been found for various measures of sexual behaviour, and the hybrids between two of the strains showed heterosis for three of fourteen behavioural measures (McGill and Blight, 1963).

Audiogenic seizures. An audiogenic seizure is a convulsion caused by a massive discharge of motor neurones in a relatively unco-ordinated pattern. They can be induced by exposing a susceptible subject to intense high-pitched sound. Differences in susceptibility of different strains of rats and mice have been found (see Fuller and Thompson, 1960, for references). Various genetic models have been postulated, but those based on multifactorial genetic control seem to fit the experimental data better than those based on one or two loci (Broadhurst, 1960). The genetic control of audiogenic seizures has also been shown by responses to selection for susceptibility to seizures.

4) *Emotionality*. A number of studies of emotional behaviour have been carried out in rodents. Thus an analysis by Broadhurst and Jinks (1961) of Dawson's (1932) data on the inheritance of wildness in mice giving a reasonable degree of heritability was presented in Section 3.5. Measures of aggression and timidity also show some genetic control. Other measures of emotionality consist of the frequency of urination and defecation during test periods, for which between strain differences have been found in rats and mice. Hall (1951) selected for high and low rates of urination and defecation in rats and produced two lines, which he called 'emotional' and 'non-emotional'. It is interesting to note that the 'emotional' line is less susceptible to audiogenic seizures than the 'non-emotional' line. Broadhurst (1960), in a very comprehensive study in rats, selected successfully for high and low defecation scores, producing two lines which he called reactive and non-reactive. Ambulation scores varied with defecation scores as pointed out previously (see Section 4.2). Many other traits varied between lines, including susceptibility to audiogenic seizures, which was changed as in Hall's lines.

5) *Fighting behaviour*. Related to emotionality is the question of fighting behaviour. Ginsburg and Allee (1942) studied fights between three inbred strains of mice, namely C-57 blacks, C-3– agoutis, and C albinos. Male mice were put together in pairs made up of individuals of different strains. For fighting ability C-57 were superior, C-3– intermediate, and C the least effective.

Studies within strains showed that there are environmental effects, in that individual mice may be conditioned to be less ag-

gressive as a result of repeated defeats, and can be more aggressive
as a result of continued victories over submissive mice. Both types
of conditioning strongly affect the ability of a given mouse to secure
or maintain high social status. Other relevant non-heritable factors
are physiological state such as fatigue and temperature, and differences in weight in that the heavier mouse wins rather more often.
Early experience is important, thus male mice raised alone and
periodically allowed to investigate each other will begin to fight at
about thirty-six days, while males which are raised together in the
same cage and left undisturbed do not begin fighting until later (see
Scott and Fredericson, 1951).

These and other experiments show the complexity of the environment, and emphasize that the raising of animals in a uniform
environment is of the utmost importance for genetic work.

Sexual selection. Turning now to studies on sexual selection of the
type discussed in Chapter Five, there is very little work compared
with *Drosophila*. Levine (1958) paired a male mouse of an inbred
albino strain ST/J with a male of an inbred black-agouti strain
CBA/J. After forty-eight to seventy-two hours an albino female was
placed with the pairs of males, and thereafter the three mice re-
mained together. It was found that 76% of the litters were fathered
solely by albino males, 12% by black-agouti males, and 12% were
mixed due to double inseminations. Using the same technique,
Levine and Lascher (1965) took pairs of males of an inbred black
strain C57BL and a brown strain C57BR. Each pair was placed in a
cage with a brown female. It was found that 70% of litters were sired
by black males, 16% by brown males, and 14% were the result of
double inseminations. Thus in both cases, one type of male had a
clear advantage over the other, so far as success in mating is concerned indicating sexual selection.

The likely explanation of these results is social dominance as is
achieved by fighting, leading to reproductive dominance. Thus
Levine (1958) reported that in twenty-seven fights observed, the
albino (ST/J) male was the victor, while in only two cases was the
black-agouti (CBA/J) male the victor. Similar observations were
made by Levine and Lascher (1965), where the black (C57BL)
male was the victor in nine fights out of ten. Thus there is a clear

correlation in both cases between victories in fights and success in reproduction.

In a further experiment Levine, Barsel, and Diakow (1965) used the somewhat different technique of placing albino (ST/J) and black-agouti (CBA/J) males together in the presence of a female in oestrus. Under these circumstances the black-agouti males were superior in both fighting ability and mating success, which is the converse of Levine's (1958) results. The presence of the female in oestrus thus forms a substantial and important environmental factor.

Successful aggressive behaviour is often a necessary prelude to sexual behaviour and acts to exclude passive males from reproduction. However, studies in mice have given contradictory results, and in some cases no correlation between the two types of behaviour was found (see Levine, Barsel, and Diakow, 1965, for discussion). Further experiments are needed, especially with a view to defining exactly the types of behaviour elicited in different experimental situations.

An apparatus described by Mainardi, Marsan, and Pasquali (1965 a) seems of particular value in this type of work. It consists of a box subdivided into three compartments in a row, each having the same dimensions. Adjoining compartments are connected with each other by holes of such a size that mice with a yoke round the neck cannot pass through the holes, but mice without a yoke can. The experimental technique consists of placing a male in the central compartment without a yoke, and a female with a yoke in each of the two lateral compartments. The male can then freely choose a female, and the time spent with each female is ascertained by a pen recorder on rotating paper. This is made possible by placing the box on a pivot, so that it moves according to the location of the male. An exactly analogous method can be used for one female with two males. The distinction between this and the previous experiments is that fighting between animals of the same sex is eliminated. Other modifications of this design are also possible, and have been described by Mainardi and his colleagues.

In one experiment using this technique, sexual preferences were studied between two strains of mice, using the male choice situation. It was found that there were no sexual preferences, and that the male preferences were determined by the different degrees of receptivity of females (Mainardi, Marsan, and Pasquali, 1965 *b*).

A further experiment is particularly important. Young mice were reared by parents perfumed with an absolutely foreign odour, an extract of *Viola odorata*, and the sexual behaviour of offspring which were allowed to choose between two individuals of the opposite sex, one perfumed and one normal, was studied. It was found that the females exerted a strong choice, but the males did not. Thus females reared by perfumed parents tended to choose perfumed males, and control females tended to choose control males. Hence the sexual preferences of female mice are strongly influenced by the precocious learning of the parents' traits. It can be assumed that olfactory stimuli are of paramount importance, since all mice belonged to the same strain. Thus it is clear that sexual preferences can be altered environmentally, in this case according to the parental traits (Mainardi, Marsan, and Pasquali, 1965 *a*).

It is curious that avoidance by females of the subspecies *Mus musculus domesticus* of males of the subspecies *bactrianus* depends on an infantile learning process, such that if females are reared by the mother alone the avoidance is annulled but not if females are reared by both sexes. Considering preferences between strains within the subspecies *domesticus*, the same sort of learning process seems to operate, such that if reared by both mother and father, females show a preference for another strain, but this is annulled if the females are reared by their mothers only. Early learning of the traits of the father, which are probably odours, seems necessary to determine the sexual preferences (see Mainardi, Marsan, and Pasquali, 1965 *a*). It will be of interest to look in more detail at other species complexes, e.g. the mouse *Peromyscus maniculatus* where sexual isolation occurs between *P. m. blandus* from New Mexico and *P. m. leucocephalus* from a Florida island in experimental populations (see Fuller and Thompson, 1960, for a recalculation of data of Blair and Howard).

Thus sexual preferences can be determined by the phenotype of a relative (imprinting) and will lead to a form of non-random mating. Imprinting based on relatives has been found in various birds such as certain duck species and the domestic pigeon. Thus from the population point of view, the assumption of random mating may break down. Furthermore, the possibility of complications due to such factors cannot be ignored when attempting to analyse the genetic component of a behavioural trait.

Learning ability. The importance of learning by experience in fighting and sexual preferences has been stressed already, and we now ask whether learning ability itself is heritable.

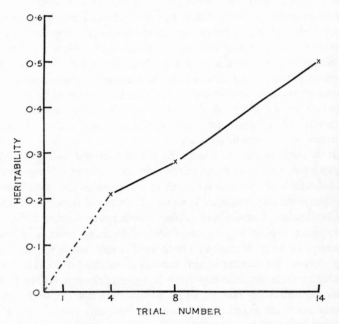

FIG. 6.1 Heritability of running time in mice plotted against trial number. (From data of Vicari recalculated by Broadhurst and Jinks, 1963.)

Using a simple maze in which subjects ran to a food reward, Vicari (1929) studied reaction times and degrees of learning in mice for four inbred strains and certain F_1s and F_2s. Characteristic differences in reaction times were obtained, and the slope of the learning curves differed. For one measure of learning, the mean running time, it is extremely interesting that the first trial gave a heritability (calculated by Broadhurst and Jinks, 1963) not significantly different from zero, and it rose regularly trial by trial (Fig. 6.1), as if there is a progressive release of a genetically determined response from the effect of environmental stimuli irrelevant to it, but which tend to obscure its action in the early stages of training. This represents one of the few examples showing the intricate interplay of hereditary and environmental determinants of behaviour.

Various selection experiments have been carried out for maze brightness and maze dullness. The best-known work is that of Tryon (1942 – see Broadhurst and Jinks, 1963; Fuller and Thompson, 1960) in rats, who selected over twenty-two generations and formed maze-bright and maze-dull lines. Unfortunately detailed genetic analyses have not been carried out, although Broadhurst and Jinks (1963) calculated a heritability in the broad sense of about 40%, using the F_1 and F_2 crosses between the lines. The data are unsatisfactory in that there is a significant genotype $\times$ environment interaction which could not be scaled out. Various other selection experiments differing in techniques are mentioned by Fuller and Thompson (1960), including some experiments with negative results. However, on the whole, the evidence indicates that maze brightness and dullness can be selected, and this provides evidence for a degree of genetic control, but it is not possible to be more definite.

Another form of learning, the conditioned avoidance response, has been studied in mice by Collins (1964), who set up a complete 5×5 diallel cross based on five inbred strains of mice and their hybrids. Testing was carried out at 100 days based on 200 trials per individual. An electric shock was delivered to a grid floor five seconds after a buzzer was turned on. A jumping response across the continuously charged pit in the first five seconds activated a photosensitive control system postponing shock for that trial and was considered an avoidance response. The number of avoidances in 200 trials made up the score for each individual. Heterosis was usual for the hybrids, and significant general and specific combining abilities were found indicating additive genes and dominance. The genetic control of a trait of this type in the rat is shown by selection experiments carried out by Bignami (1965).

Conclusions. All the traits surveyed are controlled partly genetically; however, the experimental designs used do not generally permit analyses of any sophistication, such as have been carried out in *Drosophila*, but the next few years may rectify this. It may be expected that studies on the interrelationships of behavioural traits will be carried out with increasing frequency, in an attempt to define the complete behavioural phenotype with correlated physiological variants. The selection experiment approach is particularly valuable, since in an experiment set up in which a given trait is selected, other traits can be followed to detect correlated responses to selection, as in Broadhurst's (1960) experiment where he selected for defecation scores in rats and studied ambulation scores each generation as a correlated response (Section 4.2). Eysenck and Broadhurst (1964) gave the results on these lines of over fifty tests, some behavioural and some physiological, many of which show correlated responses. Most of the correlated responses agree with what would be predicted from the dichotomy of emotionality occurring in the high (reactive) and low (non-reactive) defecation lines. If such work is combined with an attempt to seek details of correlated biochemical alterations, the possibility of finding a biochemical as well as a genetic basis for behaviour arises.

There is a similarity between behavioural and other quantitative traits such as viability, fecundity, longevity, etc., in showing heterosis between inbred strains. The organisms under study are outbreeders. Thus their genetic architectures are adapted to outbreeding, so that a high level of heterozygosity is favoured by natural selection. On inbreeding the forced increase in homozygosity generally leads to a fall in fitness, as genotypes not usually exposed to natural selection will become frequent. When two different inbred strains are crossed, the F_1 will be highly heterozygous because inbred strains are usually homozygous at different loci. This restitution of heterozygosity favoured under outbreeding often leads to heterosis. Thus behavioural heterosis does not represent a new phenomenon, but is to be expected on the basis of our knowledge of the breeding system of organisms, provided it can be assumed that the traits in question contribute to the overall fitness of the organism.

Finally, the importance of previous experience is shown in some of the experiments on fighting ability, sexual preferences, and learning. Such influences, which are probably made up of a complex interaction between genotype and environment, may have important effects on the structure of populations, especially when considering sexual preferences. Furthermore, it can be stressed again that the successful study of quantitative behavioural traits depends on eliminating such interactions, or if this is not possible, on controlling and estimating them.

6.3 *Behavioural traits with a biochemical basis*

In this section two systems will be discussed, namely alcohol consumption variations, and aspects of aromatic amino acid metabolism variations that affect behaviour and have some genetic basis. There is a vast literature on chemical substances affecting behaviour (see, for example, Eiduson *et al.*, 1964; Meier, 1963), however much of this evidence is only peripherally suggestive of a relationship between genes, biochemistry, and behaviour. Even so the investigation of this relationship will probably form an important future field of research as will be shown by the examples to be discussed.

Alcohol consumption in mice. In one series of experiments (Rodgers and McClearn, 1962 *a*) four inbred strains of mice were offered simultaneously *ad lib.* choices of water and six alcohol solutions ranging in strength from 2·5% to 15% over a three-week period. In Table 6.1 the mean daily consumption of water and the various alcohol solutions in millilitres, and the proportion of the liquid consumed that was alcohol, are given for each week. This last figure provides a single index representative of the alcohol preference of each strain on a weekly basis. In each week the rate of alcohol consumption is in the order C57BL > C3H/2 > BALB/c > A/3. For strains C57BL and C3H/2 the percentage of alcohol consumed increased over a three-week period, a marked preference for 10% alcohol developing by the third week. In strains BALB/c and A/3, however, there was a progressive reduction in alcohol consumed, and the development of an increasing preference for water. Thus in the strains tested, the tendency for alcohol preference to increase is positively correlated with initial preference. An analysis of variance of

TABLE 6.1 Mean daily consumption of various alcohol solutions (ml.), and the proportion of absolute alcohol consumed to total liquid on a weekly basis

(After Rodgers and McClearn, 1962 a)

Strain	Week	Mean daily consumption of various alcohol solutions (ml.)								Proportion of absolute alcohol to total liquid
		0·0%	2·5%	5·0%	7·5%	10·0%	12·5%	15·0%	Total	
C57BL	I	1·88	1·83	1·75	1·17	1·81	3·90	2·55	14·89	0·085
	II	1·19	0·78	1·69	3·24	1·38	4·33	2·90	15·51	0·093
	III	1·31	0·72	0·46	0·80	5·22	3·04	3·66	15·21	0·104
C3H/2	I	2·64	2·52	3·00	2·62	2·24	1·80	1·29	14·82	0·065
	II	2·44	2·29	3·96	2·34	2·84	1·36	1·32	16·55	0·066
	III	2·57	1·41	2·71	1·93	5·72	3·11	1·34	18·79	0·075
BALB/c	I	10·03	0·65	0·66	0·58	0·85	0·56	0·82	14·15	0·024
	II	9·76	0·42	0·42	0·39	0·38	0·48	0·42	12·27	0·019
	III	9·30	0·31	0·40	0·43	0·40	0·40	0·47	11·71	0·018
A/3	I	10·20	0·96	0·72	0·52	0·44	0·59	0·46	13·89	0·021
	II	11·16	0·53	0·67	0·41	0·36	0·43	0·40	13·96	0·016
	III	10·85	0·36	0·31	0·41	0·41	0·44	0·39	13·17	0·015

the proportions of liquid consumed that was alcohol on the weekly basis, revealed a highly significant effect due to different strains (genotypes), and computing components of variance showed that the differences between genotypes amounted to 97·3% of the total variability. Clearly alcohol preference is genotypically controlled, but it does depend on the environment in that alcohol preference varies according to the period of previous consumption.

Other investigations have shown a correlation between strain means for alcohol preference and liver alcohol dehydrogenase (ADH) activity (Rodgers et al., 1963). McClearn et al. (1964) took two strains, C57BL with a high alcohol preference, and DBA/2 with a strong alcohol avoidance; the former having high and the latter low ADH activity. Using these strains they studied the effects on liver ADH activity of forced alcohol consumption with 10% alcohol as the only liquid source, over various periods of time followed in some cases by forced water consumption. Results were obtained as in Fig. 6.2. There was a large difference between strains, but superimposed on this was an increase in ADH activity as a factor of alcohol consumption. Thus the highest ADH activity in both strains was obtained immediately following three weeks of forced alcohol consumption. Two weeks of forced alcohol consumption led to a slightly lower level. At a slightly lower level still, came a régime of two weeks of forced alcohol consumption followed by forced water consumption, thus three weeks of forced water consumption led to a slightly lower level of ADH activity than one week. The lowest level of all was for the controls where water only was consumed. It is not known whether the increase in ADH activity represents a release of inhibition, de novo synthesis of the enzyme, or some other process. Thus the level of ADH activity is determined by the genotype or strain as shown by the large difference between the two strains, and environment as shown by the effect of the previous history of alcohol consumption.

Certain crosses between strains have been carried out, thus the F_1 generations between various high and low strains have intermediate preferences. In a cross between the alcohol preferring C57BL strain and the alcohol avoiding A strain, the F_1 and F_2 means were intermediate between the parents, and backcrosses of the F_1

to the parental strains were in the expected direction, but the variance of the F_2 generation was smaller than that of the F_1, making the computation of heritability meaningless. Further data are needed to elaborate on this. Finally, maternal effects have been shown to be unimportant (Rodgers and McClearn, 1962 b).

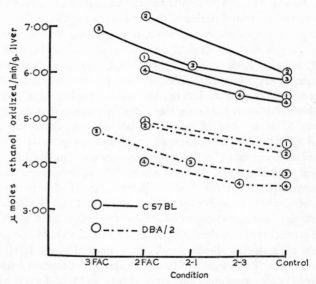

FIG. 6.2 Alcohol dehydrogenase activity under different conditions. The numbers in circles refer to different studies.

3 FAC – three weeks of forced 10% alcohol consumption

2 FAC – two weeks of forced 10% alcohol consumption

2–1 – two weeks of forced 10% alcohol consumption followed by one week of water.

2–3 – two weeks of forced 10% alcohol consumption followed by three weeks of water

Control – water only.

(After McClearn et al., 1964).

In conclusion, we have a case of a genetically controlled enzyme difference leading to a difference in behaviour. More precise genetic analyses will be awaited with interest.

Aromatic amino acid metabolism and behaviour. Aromatic amino acids act as precursors, both to pigment formation and to many vital hormones. Thus it is reasonable that in phenylketonurics in man, where there is an imbalance of phenylalanine–tyrosine metabolism, there are many metabolic abnormalities and pigmentation is affected. The imbalance of phenylalanine–tyrosine metabolism is

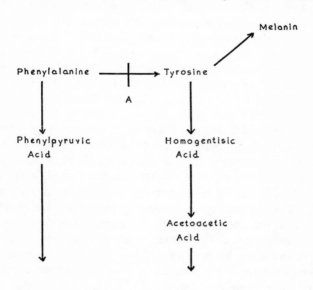

A — Block in Phenylketonurics

FIG. 6.3 Some steps in phenylalanine metabolism. Normally phenylalanine is transformed to tyrosine and various other compounds derived from tyrosine, some of which are indicated. In phenylketonurics the alternative pathway through phenylpyruvic acid assumes importance. The altered pigmentation of phenylketonurics is reasonable, because melanin formation depends partly on tyrosine.

due to the reduced activity or alteration of the enzyme phenylalanine hydroxylase, which normally converts phenylalanine to tyrosine. This leads to an accumulation of phenylalanine and hence the excretion of phenylpyruvic acid in the urine, since in phenylketonurics phenylalanine is metabolized by an alternative pathway (Fig. 6.3), compared with the normal metabolism through tyrosine. Phenyl-ketonuria is due to an autosomal recessive gene. Affected phenyl-ketonurics are modified behaviourally since they have a low I.Q. Thus there is a great interest in variations in this metabolic system in rodents and any behavioural concomitants. In rodents, the experi-mental possibilities are much greater than in man, so that informa-tion difficult to obtain in man may be sought.

Phenylalanine hydroxylase activity has been studied in some strains of mice. For example, homozygous dilute dd mice have dilute pigmentation in association with extreme nervousness, and a peculiar susceptibility to audiogenic seizures (Coleman, 1960). Another allele, dilute lethal d^1, leads to a similar dilution of pigment in homozygotes, but also affects the central nervous system so as to produce convulsive seizures followed by death at approximately three weeks of age. Some of the behavioural symptoms resulting from the presence of the dilute allele resemble phenylketonuria in man, and furthermore, pigmentation is reduced in phenylketonuric individuals. It was found on injecting phenylalanine that phenylala-nine hydroxylase activity was reduced by about a half in homozygotes dd with an intermediate level in the heterozygotes. In the dilute lethal homozygotes, d^1d^1, however, at two to three weeks of age only 14% of normal activity was shown. The influence of this gene in mice is exerted through the production of an enzyme inhibitor, which in normal mice diminishes during the third postnatal week, so that enzyme activity rises, but dilute mice retain the inhibition (see Sidman, Appel, and Fuller, 1965).

Normal laboratory rats and mice can be made phenylketonuric by overloading with phenylalanine. The diet must be commenced as soon as they are born. Excess tyrosine helps in the induction of phenylketonuria by suppressing the action of phenylalanine hydroxy-lase by over two-thirds. From the behavioural point of view, such mice take longer to run a maze than normals, that is they have a lower learning ability. They also fail to develop conditioned avoidance response behaviour, becoming non-attentive except under strong stimulation.

Feeding excess phenylalanine and tyrosine leads to a series of related substrate alterations, such as a deficiency of serotonin and catechol amines, which are important substances from the neuro-chemical point of view. When the balance of such substances is upset this may lead to mental alterations as observed in mice and man. It is, in fact, believed that the serotonin deficiency is responsible for the mental alterations rather than the concomitant deficiency of catechol amines and changes in other substrates. Biochemical alterations similar to those induced in mice have been found in phenylketonurics in man. A more complete account with references occurs in Meier (1963).

If, however, feeding is commenced after weaning, no damage to intellect is seen. In fact, a deficiency of serotonin in adult mice leads to increased learning ability, and an increase of serotonin to decreased learning ability (Woolley and van der Hoeven, 1963). This perhaps parallels the situation in man where the effects of the phenyl-ketonuria gene on I.Q. can be suppressed by feeding a diet low in phenylalanine from soon after birth, but the diet can per-haps be stopped at adolescence after the brain has completed dif-ferentiating.

Thus a metabolic defect controlled by an autosomal recessive gene in man leads to a complete 'biochemical syndrome', in terms of which attempts have been made to explain changes of mental ability. The study of this syndrome is aided by the use of different genotypes and feeding experiments in rodents. Even so, there has not been a great deal of work on the effect of different strains on biochemical vari-ability for the system, although Maas (1963) has reported differing serotonin levels in inbred strains of mice. Thus more precise analyses in rodents, where the relationship between genotype, biochemistry, and behaviour is explored, will be awaited with great interest.

Other systems. Other metabolic and physiological systems have been looked at in association with behaviour without particularly sophisticated results from the genetic point of view. Thus there seems to be a correlation between thyroid function and behaviour in rats and mice, such that emotional strains have larger thyroids than non-emotional strains. This evidence is based on inbred strains and on lines such as Broadhurst's defecation score selection lines (see Fuller, 1964). Brain cholinesterase levels have been shown to vary

I

between strains in rats, and also selection has created strains differing in brain cholinesterase levels (see Broadhurst and Watson, 1964). In view of the potential importance of this enzyme in the metabolism of chemical transmitter substances, the analysis of concomitant behavioural traits is of some importance. However, Broadhurst and Watson (1964) found little correlation of brain cholinesterase level with defecation and ambulation scores based on five inbred strains of rats.

A further approach is the investigation of heritable factors in drug response, since there are large individual differences in responses to drugs, both in man and animals (Meier, 1963; Broadhurst, 1964). Thus different inbred strains of mice show large variations in sleeping time in response to a given dose of hexobarbitone. In some of the lines derived by selection for behavioural traits, especially those of Tryon (1942) for maze brightness and dullness, and of Broadhurst (1960) for defecation scores in rats, various drugs have been shown to give drug × strain interactions for behavioural traits (Broadhurst, 1964). If it is assumed that a drug acts by affecting some metabolic pathway, then presumably we are dealing with some sort of modification of this pathway leading to a behavioural effect, and the degree of modification depends partly on the genotype. This approach will no doubt be developed very much more in the near future.

6.4 *Conclusions*

A diverse range of behavioural traits have been shown to be influenced genetically, using the biometric approach. In some cases associated physiological and biochemical bases are beginning to emerge. Although many traits have some genetic control, it is to be hoped that the approach of studying as many traits as possible in a given experiment will become common, so as to get an idea of the whole behavioural phenotype and any associated physiological and biochemical variables. Even so, it is unfortunate that rodents are so much more difficult than *Drosophila* from the point of view of precise genetic analyses. Also there is the complication of previous experience and learning, which if not under direct investigation, must be controlled. However, rodents do seem to offer at the moment, a more complex range of behavioural traits than *Drosophila*. Furthermore, there is a greater possibility of extrapolating to man where the environment cannot be controlled. These problems will be discussed further in the next chapter.

CHAPTER SEVEN

Behaviour in Man

7.1 *Introduction*

As pointed out in previous chapters, the techniques available in animals which enable a clear estimation of the relative influence of heredity and environment to be made cannot in general be applied to man, since it is virtually impossible to use completely defined genotypes and environments. This means that much of the work on behaviour in man in which clear genetic components are obvious is on traits controlled by single genes. They are traits for which the possible environmental modifications are sufficiently small, and penetrance sufficiently high that clear-cut segregations can be found in pedigrees. A further complication is that work in human behaviour genetics has often concentrated on traits of social significance, thus a great deal of information has been accumulated on intelligence with particular reference to mental defect, and on psychoses and other psychiatric problems. It is difficult to assess many of these traits objectively, so that from the genetic point of view, they are not particularly satisfactory. This contrasts with work of animal experimenters, who in general select traits because of experimental convenience, which frequently implies a reasonable level of objectivity.

Research in human behaviour genetics has therefore mainly concentrated on:

(1) The study of inheritance of traits largely under the control of one gene. In this category we can include the behavioural consequences of traits due to karyotype abnormalities.

(2) The determination of the heritability of quantitative traits, such as intelligence and personality, by using twin studies, corre-

lations between relatives and more comprehensive analyses where information from many diverse family types is obtained.

(3) As indicated in the last chapter, inferences relevant to human behaviour can be made by extrapolation from laboratory mammals, though one must be careful.

The broad aim of this chapter is to discuss the study of behaviour in man in the context of the previous chapters, with particular reference to difficulties that arise consequent upon the lack of experimental possibilities in man. A complete book in itself could be written if all the relevant work were to be reviewed, and so the approach here will be extremely selective.

7.2 Behavioural traits due to karyotype abnormalities

Since the behavioural effects of karyotype abnormalities are usually relatively clear, this seems a reasonable point at which to start.

The best-known example is that of Down's syndrome (mongolism), which is characterized by severe mental retardation, short stature, stumpy limbs, small round head, small eye openings, and various internal malformations, especially of the heart. Most individuals with the syndrome have forty-seven chromosomes, instead of forty-six the normal chromosome complement in man, due to an extra chromosome 21 or 22 which is one of the smaller somatic chromosomes. They are said to be trisomic because three members of one chromosome are present instead of the normal two. Presumably during meiosis, the chromosome pair fails to separate, so that both members of the chromosome pair enter a given gamete, and on fertilization a third member is introduced so leading to a trisomic condition. This non-disjunction of chromosomes at meiosis is probably restricted mainly to females, as the frequency of affected individuals increases rapidly with maternal age. The risk for women of forty-five is 1/50 compared with 1/3,000 for a woman of twenty. Presumably the increase in non-disjunction with age is due to a change in the environment of the oocytes induced by increasing age (see Penrose, 1963, for a detailed account of work on this syndrome).

Certain cases of Down's syndrome have forty-six rather than forty-seven chromosomes and, furthermore, often several members of a family are affected. Those with forty-six chromosomes have two chromosomes 21 and an extra long chromosome 15 suggesting that an uneven exchange of chromosome material between a chromosome 15 and 21 has occurred (that is, a translocation), so leading to a chromosome consisting of almost all of chromosome 15 plus almost all of 21 (15/21). Thus, in effect, the individual has the material of three chromosomes 21 as in affecteds due to non-disjunction. The frequent familial incidence is explained by the chromosome 15/21 occurring in normal carriers having only forty-five chromosomes. In contrast, Down's syndrome due to non-disjunction occurs sporadically. Another type of translocation in Down's syndrome concerns chromosomes of the 21, 22 group, and further origins of the syndrome are discussed by Penrose (1963).

The syndrome is probably due to an upset in the normal balance between chromosomes, since natural selection must have adapted and integrated gene activity to a situation of two representatives for each chromosome. When one pair is represented three times, as occurs by non-disjunction and occurs essentially for translocation affecteds, the result is a generalized upset in balance between chromosomes which, as a consequence, leads to the complex syndrome described.

In man, normal males are XY and females XX. In a proportion of cells of normal females, but not of normal males, there is a chromatin positive DNA body situated at the nuclear membrane. It has been postulated by Lyon (1962) and others that this chromatin body, referred to as a sex-chromatin body, represents an inactivated X chromosome. Individuals with more than one X have sex-chromatin bodies and are called sex-chromatin positive, while individuals with only one X have no sex-chromatin bodies and are sex-chromatin negative.

Sex-chromatin negative females with forty-five chromosomes have been found ('Turner's syndrome') characterized by a failure to mature sexually, and have one X chromosome only. There are also sex-chromatin positive males with forty-seven chromosomes, characterized by a failure to mature sexually ('Klinefelter's syndrome'). They are karyotypically XXY, one X being inactivated as a sex-chromatin body, so it is reasonable for them to be essentially males as they have one active X and one active Y, the Y being male determining. Sterile males karyotypically XXXY with Klinefelter's syndrome have been found, in this case with two sex-chromatin bodies in the nucleus representing two inactivated X chromosomes. Among other examples of sex-chromosome abnormalities are triple X females XXX which are usually fertile, having two sex-chromatin bodies.

These sex-chromosome number variants occur sporadically, and are probably mainly due to various types of non-disjunction. Thus no familial patterns have been found as for Down's syndrome due to translocation.

All these various conditions may be associated with some degree of mental retardation, but on the whole retardation is not as severe as that associated with Down's syndrome. At first sight this is surprising since the extra or deficient X represents a considerably larger amount of chromosomal material than the extra chromosome 21 of Down's syndrome. The likely reason for the difference resides in the in-activation of all X chromosomes above one. This type of inactivation, if it occurs for the autosomes, is probably less complete, so that the genic balance between chromosomes is more upset.

7.3 Behavioural traits largely controlled by one gene. Determination of modes of inheritance

The most direct method of examining the mode of inheritance of a trait or condition is to examine the pedigree of a family showing it and attempting to fit it to an hypothesis of dominant, recessive, or sex-linked inheritance. Under discussion here are discrete traits rather than metrical traits.

The characteristic of dominant inheritance in pedigrees is its continued transmission from parent to offspring, since a dominant condition is controlled by a gene usually present in the heterozygous form. Thus Huntingdon's chorea, which is a progressive dementia which has been traced through many generations in pedigrees, is controlled by a dominant gene (Fig. 7.1). The only difficulty is that Huntingdon's chorea has a variable age of onset, so occasional carriers do not manifest the disease probably because they die before it would have been manifested. Some other examples of conditions due to dominant genes having an effect on mental traits are: (1)

dystrophia myotonica, characterized by mental defect in association with myotonic symptoms, muscle wasting, frontal baldness, and cataract; (2) epiloia which is a syndrome of tuberose sclerosis of the brain, sebaceous adenoma, and epilepsy; (3) neurofibromatosis, in which there are multiple nerve tumours; and (4) acrocephaly which is an abnormality of head shape (Penrose, 1963).

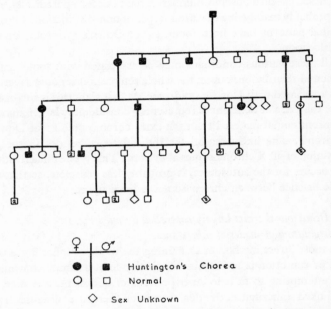

FIG. 7.1 A section of a pedigree of Huntingdon's chorea. (After Neel and Schull, 1954.)

Many traits with a behavioural component are controlled by recessive genes. In human pedigrees the study of recessive inheritance presents more difficulties than dominant inheritance, since the trait, if rare, will only occur sporadically within families, and so individual families will not reveal much about its mode of inheritance. This is because if *a* is a recessive allele and A the corresponding dominant allele, recessive homozygotes usually come from matings between two carriers of the gene *a*, thus A*a* × A*a*, from which only one-quarter of the offspring can be expected to be *aa*. This means that by chance many families in which such a mating occurs will not give an individual *aa*. Since in human families we usually detect an Aa × Aa mating from the occurrence of *aa* offspring, on a population basis there will be a bias in the overall segregation ratio due to non-segregation in families where segregation is possible. If the family size is *s*, the proportion of non-segregating Aa × Aa families will be $(\frac{3}{4})^s$. Thus the proportion of segregating families will be $1 - (\frac{3}{4})^s$, which tends to unity as *s* increases, as might be expected. Thus the bias due to non-segregating families decreases as the family size increases. Taking this into account, expected proportions of individuals with the trait can be computed and compared with the frequency observed by various methods depending somewhat on how the data are collected. Li (1961) gives an elementary discussion, and it is not proposed to discuss this complex problem further here.

Because two recessive genes must come together to show the trait under recessive inheritance, the chances of the trait appearing will be enhanced in the offspring of consanguineous marriages. Thus a greater than average occurrence of a trait in the offspring of consanguineous marriages is a strong indication of recessive inheritance. Furthermore, the rarer the trait, the more likely it is to be found in the offspring of consanguineous marriages.

There are numerous examples of rare autosomal recessive genes having an effect on behaviour, for example, phenylketonuria, which is due to a biochemical abnormality (see Section 6.3). Penrose (1963) listed a number of other conditions, which at least in some pedigrees show autosomal recessive inheritance, e.g. microcephaly and Friedrich's ataxia.

If, however, the trait is common, a random sample of the population may be selected and the occurrence of the trait within families compared with that expected on the basis of recessive inheritance. Thus preliminary results of Snyder (1932) indicated that the inability to taste phenylthiocarbamide (PTC) was controlled by a recessive gene *t*, the corresponding dominant allele being T. The problem was that of testing this mode of inheritance when the genotypes of the taster parents were unknown, being either Tt of TT.

The solution is based on the application of the Hardy–Weinberg Law which assumes random mating (Section 2.3). Letting p be the frequency of gene T and q of gene t, it is clear that the proportion of non-tasters is q^2, from which q can be obtained and hence p. Using such gene frequencies, the segregations obtained in the various possible marriage classes can be tested for goodness of fit based on

TABLE 7.1   Results of the various possible types of marriages for the taste-testing locus assuming random mating

(a) *In Theory*

Marriages	Frequency	Offspring Tasters	Offspring Non-tasters
(1) *Taster* × *Taster*			
TT × TT	p^4	p^4	
TT × Tt	$4p^3q$	$4p^3q$	
Tt × Tt	$4p^2q^2$	$3p^2q^2$	p^2q^2
(2) *Taster* × *Non-Taster*			
TT × tt	$2p^2q^2$	$2p^2q^2$	
Tt × tt	$4pq^3$	$2pq^3$	$2pq^3$
(3) *Non-Taster* × *Non-Taster*			
tt × tt	q^4		q^4
Total	1	$p^2 + 2pq$	q^2

(b) *Data of Snyder (1932)*

	Tasters	Non-tasters
(1) *Taster* × *Taster* (425)		
Observed	929	130
% Observed	87·7	12·3
% Expected	87·6	12·4
(2) *Taster* × *Non-Taster* (289)		
Observed	483	278
% Observed	63·4	36·6
% Expected	64·6	35·4
(3) *Non-Taster* × *Non-Taster* (86)		
Observed	5*	218
% Observed	2·1	97·9
% Expected	0·0	100·0

* Presumably due to illegitimacy, incomplete gene penetrance, or faulty classification on the test.

the expectations given in Table 7.1. Snyder's (1932) data (Table 7.1) which included both parents and offspring gave 2,556 tasters and 1,087 non-tasters. Thus $q^2 = 0.298$ and so $q = 0.545$. Using this value of q, the observed proportions of tasters and non-tasters in the offspring were found to be in excellent agreement with expectation for the various marriage classes (Table 7.1).

Certain rare traits with behavioural components are controlled by sex-linked recessive genes characterized in pedigrees by an excess of males with the trait, as the gene is carried on the X-chromosome and hence is exposed in the hemizygous state in males. Among rare sex-linked conditions with an effect on mental traits are sex-linked muscular dystrophy and some types of hydrocephaly. Most forms of colour blindness are controlled by sex-linked recessive genes, but are rather more common than the above conditions, so the population analysis based on random mating as described for the inheritance of the ability to taste PTC may be useful, if suitably modified to take sex-linked inheritance into account.

Single gene traits with a biochemical basis. It now seems appropriate to look in more detail at the types of traits having behavioural components which are controlled by single genes. We will commence with those traits under the control of a primary biochemical abnormality. For a more detailed discussion with a more complete list, the reader is referred to Eiduson *et al.* (1964) and Hsia (1959). Two conditions, galactosaemia and porphyria, will be briefly discussed. A third, phenylketonuria, was discussed in Section 6.3.

Galactosaemia is a rare hereditary condition controlled by an autosomal recessive gene leading to a metabolic block in the normal conversion of galactose to glucose, due to a deficiency of the enzyme galactose-1-phosphate uridyl transferase. The disease appears in infancy and is characterized soon after milk feeding commences by lethargy, cirrhosis of the liver, cataracts, and mental retardation. Chemically there is an accumulation of galactose in the plasma and its excretion in the urine. Amino-aciduria is a common feature of the syndrome. The reason why a block in the normal conversion of galactose to glucose should lead to mental retardation is unknown. However, no long-term ill effects of the disease result if a diet free from galactose or lactose is given to the infant in the first few weeks of life. Thus a knowledge of the biochemistry of the condition enables the prevention of concomitant mental retardation.

Porphyria is a class of metabolic disorders due to upsets in porphyrin metabolism (see Kalow, 1962). There are two main groups, namely the erythropoietic and hepatic porphyrias. Erythropoietic porphyria is rare and without behavioural disorders, and affected individuals die young. It is probably caused by a recessive gene and accounts for only about 1% of the described porphyrias. Biochemically it is characterized by large amounts of the normally scarce uroporphyrin I in the bone marrow and excreta leading to severe light sensitivity so that blisters readily occur.

Hepatic porphyria has a much later onset, and is a much commoner and more heterogeneous condition than the erythropoietic type. The biochemical defect seems to be an overproduction of porphyrins or their precursors in the liver, and mental symptoms may occur. There are two main types of the condition, the Swedish and South African, both inherited as autosomal dominant traits. In the Swedish type there are episodes of abdominal pain, skin lesions, and peripheral neuritis. The South African form is similar, but barbiturates render affected individuals liable to an attack, and general anaesthesia with pentothal is very dangerous.

In the case of conditions with a clear metabolic basis, there is the possibility of treatment by biochemical means. As we have seen, both phenylketonuria and galactosaemia can be alleviated by diets instituted early in infancy. In the future, treatments for more metabolic disorders may be expected as our biochemical knowledge becomes more complete. McKusick (1964) has given a series of possible treatments for genetic disorders, which range from the elimination of toxic compounds from the diet as in galactosaemia and phenylketonuria, dietary supplementation, avoidance of certain drugs as in the South African form of hepatic porphyria, and the replacement of the missing gene product.

Single gene traits without a clear biochemical basis. Some of the genetically controlled conditions cited already include morphological and behavioural disturbances without an obvious biochemical disturbance. There is also a large miscellaneous category of morphological disturbances where the modes of inheritance are not particularly clear. Many of these are present at birth and have associated mental defects often of an extremely severe degree. Thus there are gross abnormalities of the nervous system such as anencephaly, hydrocephaly, and spina bifida, probably all originating within the first eight weeks of embryonic life. Although the modes of inheritance are often obscure, in some instances anencephaly and spina bifida are caused by recessive genes, and hydrocephaly by sex-linked genes.

Thus, for conditions with a morphological rather than a biochemical basis, the mode of inheritance may be rather obscure, probably because we are farther from the primary gene product than in the case of conditions with an obvious biochemical basis. In fact, at this level there are a number of environmental factors that may lead to abnormality, for example, radiation, chemical agents, foetal infection, and birth injury. These complications mean that pedigree studies should be combined with the biometrical methods to be discussed in the next section. The other point is that with the increasing level of environmental influence, a given condition may be determined genetically, or environmentally, in which case it is called a phenocopy. It is known from work on other organisms that the likelihood of phenocopies from a given environmental stimulus depends to some extent on the background genotype. Phenocopies of conditions with an obvious biochemical basis are probably fairly rare (although see Section 6.3 for the induction of phenylketonuria in mice), but for morphological conditions are probably more common. This is because the normal development of complex morphological traits depends on many processes and reactions, so offering many possibilities for interference by environmental factors. Thus the occurrence of conditions with a rather obscure genetic origin can often be regarded as dependent on a complex relationship between heredity and environment.

Finally there are purely behavioural conditions such as the mental illnesses, some being partly under genetic control, such as epilepsy, schizophrenia, and manic-depressive psychosis. Family studies provide evidence for genetic control for these conditions, but the possibility of variation due to the environment and from interactions between genotype and environment presents difficulties, which can be partly resolved by using the biometrical methods to be discussed in the next section.

7.4 *The inheritance of quantitative traits*

We will commence with a discussion of twins, followed by a brief reference to the study of relationships between relatives (see Section 3.7), and finally the more comprehensive analysis of Cattell (1965), which attempts to use and combine information from many diverse family types, will be outlined.

Twins. Twins may be monozygotic (MZ) derived from the splitting of a single fertilized ovum, or dizygotic (DZ) derived from the fertilization and development of separate independently formed ova. Because the ovum divides after fertilization in MZ twins, they contain identical sets of genes and are commonly called identical twins, although this does not imply complete phenotypic identity, since most traits are determined by heredity and environment, and perhaps by an interaction between heredity and environment. From the genetic point of view, dizygotic twins are no more alike than are full sibs, so are commonly called fraternal or non-identical twins. However, taking into account the common prenatal environment of DZ twins and remembering that they usually grow up together, they will be expected to be more alike than sibs born at different times.

Since in studying a trait, we will make the assumption that all differences between MZ twins have an environmental origin, while differences between DZ twins arise from both environmental and genetic causes, the diagnosis of zygosity is of critical importance. In general, if twins differ in sex or any other known inherited trait having complete penetrance such as many of the blood groups, then they cannot be MZ twins. However, if the twins are alike in sex and other traits classified they need not necessarily be identical, but based on a number of simply inherited traits a probability statement concerning zygosity may be made. The derivation of the probabilities will depend on whether the genotypes of the parents are known, in which case exact probabilities of twins being alike can be computed from the genotypes of the parents and twins (taking into account other relatives where they identify heterozygotes). If, however, the parental genotypes are not known, probabilities can be worked out assuming the gene frequencies characteristic of the population to which the twins belong. Clearly, the more genetic markers that are available the more reliable will any probability statement be. Blood groups are particularly suitable as traits, and certain quantitative traits such as dermatoglyphic patterns have been found to be useful.

If under a given environment both members of a twin-pair develop the same phenotype for a discrete trait, they are said to be *concordant*, and if they have differing phenotypes they are said to be *discordant*. For a single gene difference where the environment does not appreciably affect gene expression, for example, the ABO blood groups, MZ twins would be always concordant, and DZ twins would be either concordant or discordant to the same extent as single-born sibs. This expected difference in concordance has been used as a measure of the proportion of phenotypic variability attributable to heredity. An estimate of heritability is given by:

$$H = \frac{\text{CMZ} - \text{CDZ}}{100 - \text{CDZ}},$$

where CMZ and CDZ are the percentages of concordant MZ and DZ twins respectively. H can vary between 0 and 1 in an analogous way to the heritability discussed in Chapter Three, however, we do not here use the symbol h^2 as used in Chapter Three because H and h^2 are defined rather differently. For a completely heritable trait CMZ = 100%, giving $H = 1$, and for a trait determined largely environmentally such as an infectious disease, CMZ $\approx$ CDZ giving $H \approx 0$. As an example, Neel and Schull (1954) give data for spina bifida from a paper by Gedda for which thirteen out of eighteen MZ twin pairs and twelve out of thirty-six DZ pairs were concordant, giving $H = 0.583$. For Down's syndrome sixteen out of eighteen MZ twin pairs and four out of sixty DZ pairs were concordant, giving $H = 0.881$. The value for spina bifida indicates a fair degree of genetic control as already suggested, while that for Down's syndrome a much higher degree, which is reasonable as it usually is a trisomic condition due to non-disjunction in the mother, so giving a high value for CMZ.

If the twin data consist of measurements such as height, weight, or I.Q., the method of intra-class correlation coefficients can be used to compute heritabilities (Fisher, 1950; Neel and Schull, 1954). Let V_{MZ} be the variance of the MZ twin pairs, that is, half the mean of the squares of the differences between their measurements, and let V be the total variance of the whole set of measurements calculated in the ordinary way irrespective of pairing, then it turns out that (Neel and Schull, 1954):

$$1 - r_{MZ} = \frac{V_{MZ}}{V},$$

where r_{MZ} is the intra-class correlation for MZ twins. If the twin pairs are exactly alike their mean differences would be zero, so that $V_{MZ} = 0$, and hence r_{MZ} would be 1. Conversely, as V_{MZ} approaches V, so r_{MZ} approaches 0. For DZ twins there is an analogous formula:

$$1 - r_{DZ} = \frac{V_{DZ}}{V}.$$

For the appraisal of heredity and environment for a quantitative trait the expression:

$$H = \frac{V_{DZ} - V_{MZ}}{V_{DZ}},$$

is a measure of heritability, since it provides an estimate of the proportion of variation due to heredity for the trait concerned. If this ratio equals 1, then $V_{MZ} = 0$, so that all variation is due to heredity, and if it equals 0, then $V_{DZ} = V_{MZ}$, so that all variation is environmental. This ratio may be rewritten in terms of intra-class correlations thus:

$$H = \frac{r_{MZ} - r_{DZ}}{1 - r_{DZ}}$$

(see Holzinger, 1929, and Neel and Schull, 1954, for details).

The existence of MZ twins that have been reared apart permits an extension of this analysis so that the effect of two different environments on the same genotype can be investigated, by comparing monozygotic twins reared apart (MZA) with those reared together (MZT). If r_{MZA} and r_{MZT} are the appropriate intra-class correlations, then an estimate of the proportion of the phenotype ascribable to environment, that is the effect of differing environments on the same genotype, is given by:

$$E = \frac{r_{\text{MZT}} - r_{\text{MZA}}}{1 - r_{\text{MZA}}} = \frac{V_{\text{MZA}} - V_{\text{MZT}}}{V_{\text{MZA}}}.$$

Neel and Schull (1954) presented some data of Newman, Freeman, and Holzinger (1937) as follows:

Trait	r_{MZA}	r_{MZT}	r_{DZ}	E	H
Height	0·969	0·932	0·645	−0·544	0·808
Weight	0·886	0·917	0·631	0·272	0·775
I.Q.	0·670	0·881	0·631	0·639	0·678

All show quite high heritabilities. The number of pairs in the MZA sample was nineteen, so it is not surprising that $E < 0$ for height. It is notable that the highest value of E is for I.Q., so indicating the difficulty of disentangling heredity and environment for mental traits.

There are some points that must be borne in mind when carrying out twin studies. A homogeneous sample of adequate size is of critical importance. All pairs should be derived from the same population as defined, for example, by age, culture, and geographical location. The best method of selection is from a total registry of twin births. If persons selected in adult life are those identifying themselves as twins, those selected are likely to have maintained close contacts with their co-twins, which could bias any environmental components computed.

The twin method affords the recognition of the possible hereditary basis for phenotypic differences, but not an analysis of the genotypes responsible. In some circumstances a reasonable assessment of environmental factors can be made. A source of bias is that identical twins at birth frequently exhibit larger differences in size and vigour than would be expected from their genetic identity (Stern, 1960). A much more difficult source of bias to deal with is, however, the likelihood of the greater similarity of post-natal environments of identical twins compared with non-identical twins so inflating estimates of heritability, since in general it is difficult to estimate the effect of the environment. This is one reason why it is often possible to make more accurate statements on behaviour, using experimental animals where such environmental complications can be controlled.

Relationships between relatives. This approach was described in Section 3.7, and is in general difficult to apply to behaviour in man because of non-genetic factors common to families being confounded with the common portion of their genotype, so inflating estimates of heritability. This applies particularly to methods for correlations between full sibs. The same problem occurs, of course, in the methods for estimating heritabilities from twin data. Thus there is a need to isolate and estimate such interactions between heredity and environment and this problem will now be considered.

Multiple abstract variance analysis (MAVA). Cattell (1953, 1960, 1965) has proposed that the classical analyses based on twins as described above should be abandoned for his Multiple Abstract Variance Analysis (MAVA) method, which provides a more general method for determining the influences of heredity and environment. Essentially it derives certain required abstract or hypothetical variances and correlations between sources of variance, from a set of simultaneous equations, by equating some directly observable variance to combinations of the appropriate abstract quantities. Thus the observed variance for sib pairs reared together V_{ST} can be written:

$$V_{\mathrm{ST}} = V_{wg} + V_{we} + 2r_{wg \, . \, we}\sqrt{V_{wg} \, . \, V_{we}},$$

where the abstract variances are V_{wg} the within-family genotypic variance, V_{we} the within-family environmental variance, and $r_{wg \, . \, we}$ is the correlation of these sources of variance. Several equations of this nature can be set up based on observed variances, of which eight main ones have been used so far, namely:

(1) Identical twins reared together.
(2) Identical twins apart.
(3) Sibs together.
(4) Sibs apart.
(5) Half-sibs together.
(6) Half-sibs apart.
(7) Unrelated children reared in the same family.
(8) Unrelated children reared apart.

Each will yield a simultaneous equation from which various abstract quantities can be estimated. A number of equations and solutions are given by Cattell (1960).

The method provides information on the correlation of heredity and environment, and because several diverse family types are employed, has more significance for the general nature–nurture problem than twin studies. It is capable of extension to include many variables of possible psychological importance such as order of birth, sex of siblings, variations in age of subjects and parents, and cultural subgroups. It is primarily valuable in situations where experimental control is not possible.

In Cattell's work on personality, factor scores rather than test scores are used to characterize individuals. Such scores which deal with dimensions of personality, have been established by the analysis of personality responses in rating data, questionnaire data, and objective tests. This procedure is considered by Cattell to increase reliability as compared with the use of single variables.

The collection of data is expensive, but the MAVA method has been used in a variety of personality aspects (Cattell, 1965) indicating, for example, a correlation of $+0.25$ between heredity and environment for intelligence from between-family variances. Negative correlations have been found between heredity and environment for the general level of inhibition and a neuroticism factor. Further research with these methods will be awaited with interest.

7.5 *Mental Illness*

There is a vast literature on this subject. Before commencing we must clearly distinguish between mental illness and intellectual defect. Theoretically a person with any level of intellectual capacity can suffer from any degree of mental illness, although frequently both mental illness and mental defect appear in a given syndrome. Most, if not all, of the conditions already described in this chapter represent examples of mental defect. Mental illness, perhaps more represents cases of individuals requiring care and control because they have become out of control with their social environments (Penrose, 1963). It cannot be inferred, because of the high proportion of subnormal patients having mental illness, that poor intellectual ability is a cause of mental illness.

Here we will consider three conditions with the partial aim of indicating some of the extreme difficulties in studying human behaviour at this level. The conditions are epilepsy, schizophrenia, and manic-depressive psychosis.

Epilepsy. Epilepsy is a condition characterized by convulsive seizures with loss of consciousness. Its incidence in the general population is probable about 1%. Spontaneous epileptic attacks can be regarded as either symptomatic, that is a symptom of an underlying cerebral malformation, or idiopathic where the cause is largely unknown. The symptomatic kind of epileptic attack is seen in such a condition as epiloia, and may occur in amaurotic idiocy and other progressive degenerative diseases.

In idiopathic epilepsy there seems to be an inborn tendency of dysrhythmic cerebral activity coupled with an absence of detectable structural abnormality. Intelligence is probably normal. Where there are no known physical diseases, then epilepsy itself must be regarded as a primary condition. The conditions grouped under idiopathic epilepsy are not homogeneous, so making genetical investigations difficult. Epilepsy has certainly been shown to have a familial basis, and some workers have proposed that epilepsy is controlled by a dominant gene with incomplete penetrance, or perhaps a dominant gene affected by modifier genes. Fuller and Thompson (1960) quote data of Conrad where the concordance rate for monozygotic twins was found to be 86·3%, and for dizygotics 4·1%, giving $H \approx$ 0·80. The lack of perfect concordance for MZ twins indicates that genes do not inevitably determine the disease and that there is an environmental component.

Schizophrenia. The incidence of schizophrenia in the general population has been estimated as about 1%. This disease which often sets in during the third decade of life has been called dementia praecox or early insanity. It is characterized by a cleavage in the personality which in extreme cases may necessitate placing the patient permanently in an institution.

Twin studies show concordance rates greater for MZ than for DZ twins. Combining various data, Stern (1960) has computed values of

CMZ = 80% and CDZ = 13%, giving H = 0.77. The absence of concordance in 20% of MZ twins shows the influence of the environment in the disease. As in most examples of mental illness, it can be asked whether the high rate of concordance in identical twins is due to the mental shock in one twin caused by the onset of the disease in the other. However, the data on non-identical twins show that in most cases this shock is insufficient to cause the disease. Even though it is likely that the mental reaction of an identical twin to the illness of his twin partner is different from the case of non-identical twins, it is unlikely that this difference in psychological attitude can account for the difference in concordance.

The frequency of schizophrenics in the relatives of affecteds has been worked out in several instances. In Table 7.2 are some figures

TABLE 7.2   Expectancy of schizophrenia in relatives of propositi (After data tabulated by Fuller and Thompson, 1960)

Relationship to propositus	% Expectancy
Step-sibs	1.8
Half-sibs	7.0–7.6
Full-sibs	11.5–14.3
Children:	
One parent affected	16.4
Both parents affected	68.1
Parents	9.3–10.3
Grandparents	3.9
Grandchildren	4.3
Nephews and nieces	3.9

for relatives, which can be compared with the general population incidence of 0.5–1%. The figures are all a great deal higher than the general expectancy rate and generally correlate with the degree of kinship. This is a strong indication of genetic factors in the determination of schizophrenia.

The genetic basis of schizophrenia has been the subject of much discussion. Hypotheses ranging from recessive to dominant inheritance, and to polygenic control have been put forward. In many cases a single partially dominant gene with low penetrance has been suggested as a reasonable explanation (Böök, 1959; Slater, 1958).

The penetrance of the gene on this hypothesis is about 25%, so that non-manifestation would occur in 75% of cases due to genetic background and environmental factors. If a single gene Sc is responsible, then schizophrenia represents an example of a genetic polymorphism, as it occurs too frequently to be maintained by mutation alone. Assuming random mating, its maintenance would depend on a balance of selective factors where the heterozygotes for the gene would probably be fitter than the corresponding homozygotes (see Section 2.3). Further, the fertility or reproductive fitness of schizophrenics is on average only about 70% of that found in socio-economically comparable normals. As pointed out by Huxley *et al.* (1964), the gene would be rapidly lost without a compensatory selective advantage. Two types of possible compensatory advantage have been postulated. One is physiological, since schizophrenics are very resistant to surgical and wound shock, visceral perforation, pain, arthritis, allergies, high doses of histamine, insulin, thyroxin, and other physiologically active substances, and probably to many infections. Non-penetrant Sc carriers probably enjoy similar advantages of a lower order. The second compensatory advantage is reproductive in that the fertility of female schizophrenics and of non-penetrant Sc carriers may be somewhat above average, although male schizophrenics are at a severe reproductive disadvantage.

Recent evidence (see Huxley *et al.*, 1964) indicates that the Sc gene may cause an error of metabolism, resulting in the formation of some substance interfering with the normal integration of perception. The possibility of an error in metabolism is supported by the observation that certain psychomimetic drugs will induce symptoms closely resembling schizophrenia, and from the detection of abnormal substances in the urine of many schizophrenics.

If these recent suggestions can be further substantiated, then with time a detailed biochemical basis for many schizophrenics may be found. This will bring up the possibility of its treatment by chemical means. In individuals where schizophrenia is likely to develop, treatment may possibly be carried out to prevent its expression. This may be aided by the observation that future schizophrenics may show marked personality and temperamental differences from an early age. It is likely that the next few years will advance our knowledge of schizophrenia and its inheritance from the stage where it is obvious that there is a genetic component, to the stage where the actual gene (or genes) responsible can be followed. Biometrical methods are of great importance in ascertaining a genetic component initially, but as soon as actual loci can be identified and followed, such methods become less important and can be replaced by pedigree studies.

Manic depressive psychosis. This has an incidence of just under 0·5% in the general population. It is a condition characterized by alternating emotional states of exaggerated exaltation and depression. Relatives of index cases show a higher incidence than the general population. Stern (1960) summarized several sets of twin data and arrived at CMZ = 77% and CDZ = 19%, giving $H = 0·72$. Once again there is a reasonably high heritability with an environmental component. More detailed genetic studies favour an autosomal dominant gene as responsible in many cases, but there are the usual difficulties in assessing the importance of genotype and environment.

7.6 *Intelligence and personality traits*

Intelligence. So far we have mainly considered abnormal forms of behaviour, but now we turn to intelligence in terms of which it is theoretically possible to give everyone a measure. To discuss the heritability of intelligence levels it is necessary to find a metric on which intelligence can be assessed which is independent of the environment in particular previous experience.

A commonly used test of intelligence is the intelligence quotient or I.Q., which has proved useful in many circumstances. Based on the test score the procedure is to assign a child a mental age which is divided by his real age and multiplied by 100. The average value is then, by definition, 100. The I.Q. is almost independent of age between about five and thirteen years. However, for adults it is a less valid concept. A fictitious base of about 14½ years of chronological age is used, but some workers use other bases around this figure. The distribution of I.Q. values is continuous and no specific genes affecting I.Q. have been detected, except the genes discussed earlier in this chapter which lead to mental deficiency. Various other intelligence tests have been formulated, and all give results which can be correlated with I.Q. results to a greater or less extent.

Erlenmeyer-Kimling and Jarvik (1963) carried out a literature survey on I.Q. and certain other special intelligence tests from which were calculated mean correlation coefficients between various groups of individuals reared together, namely unrelated individuals, foster parent–child, parent–child, sibs, and MZ and DZ twins, and between various groups of individuals reared apart, namely unrelated individuals, sibs, and MZ twins (Table 7.3). The correlation

TABLE 7.3   Approximate correlation coefficients between relatives reared together and reared apart for intelligence test scores

(After Erlenmeyer-Kimling and Jarvik, 1963)

	Reared apart	Reared together
Unrelated	− 0·01	0·23
Foster parent–child		0·20
Parent–child		0·50
Sibs	0·40	0·49
Twins – DZ:		
Like-sex		0·53
Unlike-sex		0·53
Twins – MZ	0·75	0·87

coefficients obtained can be assessed by comparison with the theoretical values given in Table 3.9. For those reared together, the parent–child, sib, DZ and MZ twin correlation coefficients are close to the factor by which h^2_N is multiplied in the theoretical values, thus showing a high degree of heritability for intelligence. However, the foster parent–child correlation coefficient and that for the unrelateds come to about 0·2, whereas the expected value would be 0, so showing an environmental effect. Unrelateds reared apart do, however, give a correlation coefficient of 0 as expected. The environmental effect is also shown from the lower correlation coefficient from MZ twins reared apart as opposed to those reared together, and from the lower coefficient from sibs reared apart as opposed to those reared together. Even so, in both the reared apart and reared together columns, the observed correlation coefficients do increase with the closeness of relationship, so showing a general genotypic component.

In discussing the effects of heredity and environment, studies on adopted children are useful since they provide one way of getting over the difficulty of the resemblance between relatives being due to a common family environment. However, one complication is that some adoption agencies attempt to try to match the adopting and natural parents. Results of one study due to Leahy (quoted in Stern, 1960) are given in Table 7.4 in which there was thought to be relatively little selective placement. All children were placed in their

TABLE 7.4 Mean I.Q. of adopted and 'own' children according to father's occupation
(Data of Leahy taken from Stern, 1960)

Occupation of father	Adopted children		'Own' children	
	Number	I.Q.	Number	I.Q.
Professional	43	112·6	40	118·6
Business, management	38	111·6	42	117·6
Skilled trades and clerical	44	110·6	43	106·9
Semiskilled	45	109·4	46	101·1
Relatively unskilled	24	107·8	23	102·1

foster homes before the age of six months, and were tested between the ages of five and fourteen. Among the adopted children the range of I.Q. by father's occupation is a little less than five points. In the natural children, where genetic as well as environmental influences play a part, the range is greater than seventeen points. Other studies on adopted children give similar results, even though there may have been selective placement. The evidence therefore argues for a genetic component in intelligence.

As well as correlations between parent and offspring, a regression approach can be used (Section 3.7). Thus Burt (1943) has given figures showing that the children's I.Q.s are on average between the fathers' I.Q. and that of the mean I.Q. of the population, 100 (see Penrose, 1963, for discussion). One group of fathers with an I.Q. of 117·1 had children with an average I.Q. of 109·1, and conversely, another group of fathers with an I.Q. of 86·8 had children with an average I.Q. of 92·0. Thus the children's I.Q.s regress nearly one-half of the way towards the mean of the population. A regression of one-half is exactly what one would expect based on I.Q. being determined entirely by additive genes. For sibs a similar result would be expected. For half-sibs, nephews, and nieces, which are more remote relatives, a regression three-quarters of the way towards the mean would be expected. Observed results are in good agreement (Table

TABLE 7.5 Mean I.Q. for defective patients and their relatives
(After Penrose, 1963)

	Type of relationship to patient	Number of pairs	Patients' mean I.Q.	Relatives mean I.Q.	
				Observed	Expected on additive gene hypothesis
Patients with an I.Q. ⩾ 50	Sib	101	65·8	84·9	82·9
	Half-sib, nephew, or niece	143	63·2	89·5	91·8
Patients with an I.Q. < 50	Sib	120	24·2	87·4	61·1
	Half-sib, nephew, or niece	90	33·3	95·1	83·3

7.5) for people with I.Q.s ⩾ 50. Such individuals are effectively the fertile group since fertility below an I.Q. of 50 is low.

On the other hand, if propositi are taken with an I.Q. < 50, the relatives have a considerably higher I.Q. than would be expected on the additive gene hypothesis (Table 7.5). In some cases, specific recessive or partially recessive genes are responsible, and in other cases new mutations or environmental accidents may be responsible so that additivity breaks down. Roberts (1952) has confirmed this type of result based on sibs of defectives.

Finally, the MAVA method of Cattell gave a correlation between heredity and environment of +0·25 (Cattell, 1965), and the same approach showed heredity to play a larger role than the environment for this factor (Cattell, Blewett, and Beloff, 1955). This approach will probably be valuable in future work, since it does attempt to quantify the correlation between heredity and environment from a general point of view. Our general conclusion is that intelligence is controlled by genotype, environment and genotype × environment interactions, but it is difficult to say much more except that the environmental and interaction components are likely to be more important than for purely physical traits such as height and weight.

Personality Traits. Attempts have been made to evaluate other mental traits such as temperament, emotional behaviour, and specific abilities. It is not proposed to go into any details here, except to point out that, as for intelligence, the same difficulty in objective measurement holds. Factor scores are often used in this work. Similarity of habits and interests may form strong environmental sources of resemblance in personality traits within twin pairs and families, so making the separation of genotype and environment extremely difficult. However, the MAVA method discussed in Section 7.4 offers the possibility of estimating various correlations between heredity and environment.

Eysenck (1956) developed an introversion–extroversion factor which he showed by intra-class correlations to be as much influenced by heredity as by environment. Among other traits showing heritable influences are personal tempo, psychomotor and sports activities, and neuroticism.

In any case, the complexities introduced by genotypes reacting differentially to different environments probably become so acute leading to large genotype × environment interactions, that in some cases definite conclusions are difficult to make. This, coupled with the difficulties in objective measurement, makes definitive work on personality traits in man extremely difficult.

7.7 *Sense perception*

In this section, variations in taste, vision, olfaction, and hearing will be briefly discussed, even though the conclusions are restricted to a few major loci. However, some of the approaches described in previous sections may well find increasing applications in quantitative sense-perception studies.

Considering variations in taste, a situation well known to geneticists is the observation that the inability to taste phenylthiocarbamide (PTC) is controlled by a simple recessive gene t, the corresponding dominant allele being T (Section 7.3). Most populations have more tasters than non-tasters, thus in the American white population there are about 70% tasters. This gene is thus present at a frequency too high to be maintained by mutation alone, and so represents a case of genetic polymorphism. It is likely that the polymorphism may be in some way connected with thyroid function. It must be an extremely old polymorphism, since observations on the reactions of chimpanzees to PTC solutions suggest that taste-deficiency may also occur in the apes.

The PTC taste deficiency extends to a number of related compounds. The following chemical configuration is essential.

The fact that tasters find PTC extremely bitter brings up the possibility of genetic factors in the determination of food likes and dislikes from a much more general point of view. In one survey conducted by Fischer *et al.* (1961), forty-eight subjects were tested for food dislikes and aversions on 118 foods. Percentage of foods disliked was used as the score. Taste testing for the bitter substances quinine and 6-*n*-propylthiouracil was carried out at the same time to find the concentration at which these substances were tasted. Plotting the percentage of foods disliked against increasing concentrations of bitter compounds gave a negative linear regression significant at the 0·1% level for both compounds (Fig. 7.2). Thus the lower the taste threshold for the bitter substances, the greater the number of foods disliked, so that taste-acute individuals, so far as bitter substances are concerned, like fewer foods than those less taste-acute. These results give no information on the genetic control of taste, however, there is an association between taste sensitivity for 6-*n*- propylthiouracil and PTC which indicates the likelihood of some genetic control.

Defective colour vision of the kind generally known as red–green colour blindness was recognized as early as the eighteenth century. Normal people can match colour by the addition of colours from three spectral regions, red, green, and blue. In the most severe form of red–green defect, the subjects can make colour matches with two hues only, and these are therefore known as dichromates instead of the normal trichromates. There are two types of dichromates, namely the protanopes or 'red blind', and the deuteranopes or 'green blind'. Then there are two corresponding anomalous trichromatic conditions, namely protanomaly and deuteranomaly, where affected individuals are partially red and green blind respectively. These conditions are all controlled by sex-linked recessive alleles perhaps at two closely linked loci, one for the 'red blind' alleles and the other for the 'green blind' alleles. The frequency of the

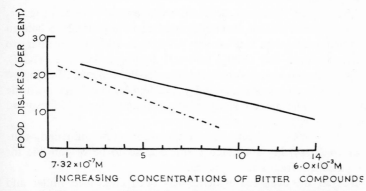

FIG. 7.2 Linear regression of the percentage of foods disliked against thresholds for 6-*n*-propylthiouracil and quinine. Numbers on the abcissa are concentrations of 6-*n*-propylthiouracil (——) and quinine (—·—), each step representing a doubling of the concentration. (After Fischer *et al.*, 1961.)

conditions is therefore much higher in males than in females. The frequency of colour-blind males varies from population to population but may be as great as 10%, which is far too high to be maintained by mutation alone, and so constitutes a case of genetic polymorphism, although as yet there is little clear idea as to the selective factors involved.

From the physiological point of view there is evidence in protanopes for a lack of photosensitive pigments in the red cones of the retina, and in deuteranopes for a defect in the cone type which contains both red and green sensitive pigments.

As well as the above conditions, there is a rare dichromatic defect, tritanopia and the corresponding tritanomaly in which colour discrimination in the blue–green region is affected. Autosomal recessive inheritance seems to be involved here.

For colour-blindness studies, therefore, the specific loci involved can be located and studied, as is the case for the taste-testing locus. In both cases there is a reasonably direct link with physiological and biochemical variants. Thus there is a fairly direct link between genes and behaviour, which partly explains why these systems have come to our notice.

Little work has been done on variations in olfactory acuity, probably because of a lack of understanding of the general mechanism of odour perception. One curious example of variable sensitivity to smell concerns the ability to smell hydrogen cyanide (HCN). This is a trait probably controlled by a sex-linked gene, since in two surveys about 18% of males and 5% of females could not smell the substance. The great toxicity of the substance makes widespread testing dangerous.

Some work has been done on auditory discrimination, thus Kalmus (1949) has suggested a single locus to be responsible for tone deafness from family studies.

Not all the available evidence has been cited (see Fuller and Thompson, 1960), but it is difficult to escape the conclusion that genetic work on sense perception is limited to a few isolated cases where work of some sophistication has been carried out. Clear-cut but rare conditions, such as blindness and deafness, occur due to anatomical defects in some cases with a genetic basis; however, of much more interest is the genetic component in normal vision, taste, smell, and hearing. Especially for taste and smell where it is difficult to be objective, a great deal of extra work of a biometric nature is needed.

7.8 Assortative mating
In the derivation of correlations between relatives it was assumed that parents mate at random. As soon as there are deviations from random mating, such as inbreeding or assortative mating, then the formulae given in Section 3.7 will no longer be strictly true. In Sections 5.5 and 5.7 experimental evidence was given within species of *Drosophila* for positive assortative mating. In man as long ago as

1903, Pearson and Lee found positive correlation coefficients between partners at marriage for physical traits, such as stature and span. The coefficients were usually about 0·2. In general this has been confirmed by later work. Hence there is a tendency for similar phenotypes to mate together based on phenotypic resemblance. Assortative mating of this type is formally equivalent to inbreeding assuming a correspondence between genotype and phenotype, which is so provided that it can be assumed that the traits under study are heritable, as has been demonstrated in man from correlations between relatives and twin studies (Fisher, 1918; Clark, 1956; Spuhler, 1962).

For a single gene pair A and a assuming no dominance, assortative mating will lead to an excess of AA × AA, Aa × Aa, and aa × aa matings, and a deficiency of AA × Aa, AA × aa, and Aa × aa matings. This will lead to an excess of homozygotes so simulating inbreeding. The consequence for multiple gene models of inheritance differ from those for inbreeding in that fewer of the possible homozygous genotypes are preserved. If, for example, we have a metrical trait such as height, where A and B are genes increasing height, and a and b are genes reducing height, then the extreme genotypes will be AABB and aabb. Complete positive assortative mating would lead to these genotypes only, while continued close inbreeding would fix all homozygotes AABB, AAbb, aaBB, and aabb. Since assortative mating tends to preserve extremes, it may be regarded as a diversifying process tending to increase variability as was pointed out in Section 5.7. Even so, assortative mating has been studied rather little from a theoretical point of view until very recently (O'Donald, 1960; Parsons, 1962). For the present discussion, however, the main point is that it does occur and leads to a breakdown in the assumption of random mating.

Spuhler (1962) summarized work of his own and others on physical, psychological, and sociological traits. For physical traits, his data gave significant positive correlations at the 5% level or better for twenty-nine of forty-three traits, while twelve of the remaining fourteen were positive. It should be stressed, as was stressed by Spuhler, that some of these measurements are intercorrelated, and a multi-variate analysis would be needed to ascertain the relative independence of each measurement from every other. He also presented evidence showing the heritability of many of the physical traits based on twin studies. Thus the positive correlations must have an effect on the genetic constitution of population.

Positive assortative mating has also been found for various tests of intelligence. Thus the Progressive Matrices Test of Raven gave a correlation coefficient $r = 0.399$ $(P < 0.01)$. A test on verbal meaning based on the selection of one of four words which best completes the meaning of each of forty sentences gave $r = 0.305$ and 0.732 for the total number of right answers, and the proportion of right answers respectively. Both correlation coefficients are significant at the 1% level. Twin data gave heritabilities of 0.94, 0.45, and 0.40 for the Progressive Matrices Test, the total number of right answers in the sentences, and the proportion of right answers in the sentences respectively. The first two heritabilities are significant at the 5% level and the last is sub-significant at the 10% level. We therefore conclude that there is evidence for positive assortative mating for these various measures of intelligence, which is important from the population point of view because these measures are partly heritable. Finally, Spuhler reported on published work showing positive assortative mating for some psychological traits, namely association, neurotic tendency, and dominance, and Beckman (1962) gave data showing positive assortative mating for musical ability.

It may well be that the strongest tendency for assortative mating occurs for behavioural traits, which probably have a lower genotypic component than physical traits. This means that a high correlation between mates for behavioural traits, as is often found, may have only as much effect on the genetic constitution of the population as a lower correlation for physical traits.

There are, as with most genetic studies in man, difficulties in interpretation. If positive assortative mating is found, then it could be due to the combination of two groups, within which mating is at random, but between which mating is non-random tending to maintain the isolation of the groups. If, for example, the groups differed for height, or a trait such as eye colour, and the division into groups were ignored, then positive assortative mating would be found over the whole population simply as a result of combining two semi-discrete groups. Spurious assortative mating of this type might occur in a city with a number of discrete ethnic groups brought together by immigration. Thus we would have over the whole city a type of cultural assortative mating as found in an Australian city based on a surname analysis of those having English, Irish, and Scottish surnames (Hatt and Parsons, 1965). False positive correlations could also be obtained by lumping data from different time periods. For example, if there is a temporal increase in height over a period of, say, fifty years, then significant positive correlation coefficients for height may be obtained if the temporal change is ignored (Beckman, 1962). Similarly, false positive correlations for family fecundity measured by the number of sibs of husband and wife have been found, which are due to combining data from different time periods (Beckman, 1962). A final complication is that assortative mating may perhaps be partly imitated by imprinting, i.e. the choice of mates based on the traits of parents or relatives, and it would be of interest to collect data to test this possibility (see Section 6.2 for a discussion of imprinting in mice).

7.9 *Conclusions*

(1) The study of the inheritance of traits wholly or mainly under the control of one gene, where pedigree studies can be carried out to clearly identify genotypes, has assumed considerable importance, especially where biochemical and physiological bases for the traits are emerging.

(2) Using biometrical methods it has been shown that many quantitative behavioural traits are controlled genotypically, but estimates of heritability are often made inaccurate by interactions between genotype and environment. Future research along the lines of the MAVA (Multiple Abstract Variance Analysis) method may help to resolve this difficulty.

(3) Some of the methods of analysis for quantitative traits, such as the study of correlations between relatives, assume a random mating population, but for many traits the occurrence of assortative mating between parents could lead to errors which in some cases should be considered.

(4) There are many difficulties in the study of behaviour in man

L

which is why inferences on the genetic component of behavioural traits are much vaguer than in other organisms, with the exception of the study of rare defects.

(5) A vast field for future research lies in the detailed study of behaviour genetics in man as the difficulties mentioned in this chapter become circumvented.

CHAPTER EIGHT

Behaviour and Evolution

The traits discussed in this monograph range from those where single genes and chromosomes can be identified as having a major role, to those where the environment is of major importance. For many traits the genetic control is based on many genes, i.e. it is *polygenic*. Such traits are therefore quantitative rather than qualitative, hence the biometric approach has proved to be powerful for assessing the relative importance of heredity and environment. If behaviour, whether determined by one or many genes, were determined by the genotype alone and the environment had no effect, then this would imply inflexibility at the phenotypic level. Clearly some flexibility is desirable, so that the organism can adapt to different situations as they arise.

Polygenic control implies the action of many genes, some with large and some with small contributions to the phenotype. Furthermore, genes may show interactions both within loci (dominance) and between loci (epistasis). Genes cannot be thought of in isolation, since the fitness of a gene depends on the genetic environment in which it occurs, which may vary between organisms and populations. It is, in fact, not too extreme to say that every gene interacts with every other in its usual genetic environment. The total gene complex controlling a trait in a given population is built up by natural selection in response to the requirements for the survival of the species in the specific environment of the population under consideration. Thus gene complexes are built up to make a high contribution to the fitness of the population. Dobzhansky (1955) refers to such gene complexes as co-adapted, and in different populations within the same species the co-adapted gene complexes may vary somewhat. Mather (1943) uses the term 'balanced genotype' to describe the same phenomenon, and from theoretical considerations has postulated the types of gene arrangements and interactions that various types of natural selection would favour.

It is likely that all the behavioural traits discussed in this monograph affect the overall fitness of the organism. There seems to be no *a priori* reason for regarding any of the traits as having no contribution to fitness, however subtle. The fact that a trait may have no obvious contribution to fitness may reflect our ignorance. It is in any case extremely difficult to establish fitness factors associated with loci in both natural and artificial populations. Thus we must expect to find that many behavioural traits are under the control of co-adapted gene complexes, just as earlier studies have revealed co-adapted gene complexes controlling traits such as fecundity, viability, and capacity to increase in *Drosophila*. Unfortunately most of the work on behavioural traits so far, has been aimed at showing them to be under genetic control without further elaborations. However, some of the experiments which have revealed evidence for co-adapted gene complexes are:

(1) *Crosses between individuals from populations from different localities*
Frequently fitness falls in the hybrids because co-adapted complexes vary between localities. This has been observed in population cages of *D. pseudoobscura* by Dobzhansky and his co-workers for non-behavioural traits (see Dobzhansky, 1955). A good behavioural example is the breakdown of dominance in the polymorphism controlling wing and colour pattern in the females of the mimetic butterfly *Papilio dardanus*, when crossing butterflies from different localities (Sheppard, 1963; and Section 2.5). This would lead to a less efficient mimicry system in natural populations.

(2) *Artificial inbreeding of an outbred species*
This leads to the production of relatively homozygous genotypes not previously exposed to the action of natural selection. That is, natural selection is no longer acting on co-adapted gene complexes. This is usually accompanied by a general fall in fitness of the inbred genotypes, one manifestation of which is their increased variability. Thus the level of *developmental homeostasis* is lower in the homozygotes,

since the end-products of development are more variable than before inbreeding. This phenomenon has been observed for many fitness factors where the appropriate experiments have been carried out. Another manifestation of lowered fitness is a reduction in the ability of the organism to tolerate a wide range of environments, as has been shown for traits such as larval survival and viability in *Drosophila* (Parsons, 1959; Dobzhansky and Levene, 1955). There is some suggestive evidence for this phenomenon for mating speed and duration of copulation, comparing heterokaryotypes with homokaryotypes in *D. pseudoobscura* (Parsons and Kaul, 1966 a; Section 3.6).

(3) *Artificial selection experiments*

As with inbreeding, artificial selection for a trait will produce extreme genotypes not previously exposed to natural selection. The consequence is usually a fall in fitness, since natural selection is no longer acting on co-adapted gene complexes. As a result the population will tend to resist the selection pressure, and furthermore, when selection is discontinued there is often a tendency for the population to return to its original condition. This phenomenon, whereby the population attempts to counter, more or less, the artificial stress to which it has been subjected, is referred to as *genetic homeostasis* (Lerner, 1954) and has been observed for many traits. In their lines selected for geotaxis, Dobzhansky and Spassky (1962) found a partial loss in the response after selection was relaxed (Section 4.3). In such selection experiments on behavioural traits that have been carried out long enough, the response per generation fell after a few generations. Thus there is indirect evidence for genetic homeostasis, and co-adapted gene complexes controlling the trait before selection.

These experiments show that there are co-adapted gene complexes built up by natural selection for behavioural traits. One complication for behavioural traits is the likelihood of high variability occurring, due to fluctuations in the environment, but this problem can be overcome by using some of the experimental designs discussed in this monograph.

Looking now at interspecific variation, an intriguing class from the behavioural point of view are the sibling species (Section 5.6). There are several groups of sibling species in the genus *Drosophila*, for example, *D. melanogaster* and *D. simulans*, which are morphologically almost identical but are almost completely isolated reproductively. Thus there is substantial divergence at the behavioural level coupled with considerable morphological similarities. However, the genetic control of the developmental pathways leading to the morphological similarities differs, since in hybrids between the two species many disturbances in bristle development occur (Sturtevant, 1929). Thus the co-adapted gene complexes leading to the similar morphological phenotypes are different, implying an underlying genetic diversity. The similarity of the outward phenotypes due to different gene complexes is due to developmental homeostasis, which is upset when combining the two different co-adapted complexes in the hybrids. However, the phenotypes of the two species differ markedly at the behavioural level, so that there is no *behavioural homeostasis* corresponding to the developmental homeostasis when making comparisons between species.

These comments would not have been necessary, had it not been that taxonomy was largely developed on morphological criteria, and only more recently has the fundamental criterion of reproductive isolation become studied seriously. Also only studied recently is the problem of physiological similarities and differences between species. Thus using Australian populations, *D. simulans* has been found to be less tolerant of high and low temperatures than *D. melanogaster* (Hosgood and Parsons, unpublished). Clearly for sibling and other species, behavioural differences perhaps in association with, or arising as a result of, ecological–physiological differences, will promote isolation.

Another pair of sibling species is *D. pseudoobscura* and *D. persimilis*. Initially they were thought to be morphologically indistinguishable, but detailed studies have revealed some slight differences. However, at the ecological–physiological level, there are differences in habitat and food preferences, diurnal rhythm activity, reactions to light, and other factors (Section 5.6 and Pittendrigh, 1958). They also differ in their time of reaching sexual maturity. These factors must help to promote the almost complete reproductive isolation that is found between the species.

Thus sibling species show a high level of developmental homeostasis leading to phenotypes which are morphologically very similar, but at the physiological and behavioural level the level of homeostasis is lower. This is perhaps not so surprising since it is these traits that will determine where a species can live and will permit adaptation to micro-environments. These traits will necessarily vary between two sibling species, since in general two species cannot occupy the same niche (see Mayr, 1963, for discussion). Thus behavioural differences may arise from underlying ecological–physiological differences, which will then be perfected by natural selection so as to lead to reproductive isolation between the species, especially if they are sympatric over part of their range.

As stressed by Mayr (1963, p. 604) 'the shift into a new niche or adaptive zone is, almost without exception, initiated by a change in behaviour'. In the shift into new adaptive zones, habitat and food selection, which are behavioural phenomena, are of major importance. Thus the importance of behaviour in initiating new evolutionary phenomena is self-evident, and at least initially there will probably be only minor modifications at the structural level, although the evolution of morphological change may follow a permanent behavioural change. Mayr (1963), for example, argues that the perfection of bipedalism in the evolution of man was speeded up by the preoccupation of the anterior extremity with 'manipulation', a behavioural trait, and that the tremendous increase in brain-size during the mid-Pleistocene was caused by the development of an efficient system of communication, speech. That behavioural phenomena are so important in initiating evolutionary change may partially explain the high level of variation of behavioural traits in response to different environmental regimes compared with morphological traits.

It should be clear that behavioural traits have a highly significant role in evolution. For this reason, the study of the genotypic control of behavioural traits is an important field of research, even though it is often difficult to obtain accurate results. The ideal situation is to attempt to characterize the behaviour of an organism as an integrated whole, so as to make meaningful comparisons between populations within species, and also between species. This is extremely difficult, but is being attempted in a preliminary way in *Drosophila* and in certain rodents, where several diverse types of behaviour can be quantified reasonably objectively. Even if this is done, there is still the major problem of extrapolating from the laboratory to the natural population in its niche, where controlled environments and known genotypes do not occur. Thus what can be done in natural populations has some similarities to the problems of studying behaviour in man. However, one advantage is that the behaviour of some animals can be studied experimentally in the laboratory, to obtain detailed information on the genotypic control of traits, perhaps even to the level of individual genes. With this background, the study of behaviour in natural populations ought to be more meaningful.

In conclusion, we have the methods for studying the genetic control of some behavioural traits in certain organisms at a fairly sophisticated level in the laboratory. The next few years ought to see substantial developments along these lines. In man the difficulty of making any sort of exact statement has been continually stressed, but the level of biochemical and physiological sophistication possible in man may lead to progress. In natural populations of animals it is often difficult to do more than to state the problems, but a combined attack in the laboratory and in the wild should slowly lead to progress. Our ignorance is well summed up by Mayr (1963, p. 9): 'There are vast areas of modern biology, for instance biochemistry and the study of behaviour, in which the application of evolutionary principles is still in the most elementary stage.' This monograph is an attempt at applying evolutionary principles to behaviour.

References

BARKER, J. S. F. 1962. Studies of selective mating using the yellow mutant of *Drosophila melanogaster*. *Genetics*, **47**, 623–40.

BASTOCK, M. 1956. A gene mutation which changes a behavior pattern. *Evolution*, **10**, 421–39.

BATEMAN, A. J. 1949. Analysis of data on sexual isolation. *Evolution*, **3**, 174–7.

BEARDMORE, J. A., DOBZHANSKY, TH., and PAVLOVSKY, O. A. 1960. An attempt to compare the fitness of polymorphic and monomorphic experimental populations of *Drosophila pseudoobscura*. *Heredity*, **14**, 19–33.

BECKMAN, L. 1962. Assortative mating in man. *Eugenics Rev.*, **54**, 63–7.

BIGNAMI, G. 1965. Selection for high rates and low rates of avoidance conditioning in the rat. *Animal Behaviour*, **13**, 221–7.

BIRCH, L. C. 1955. Selection in *Drosophila pseudoobscura* in relation to crowding. *Evolution*, **9**, 389–99.

BÖÖK, J. A. 1959. Genetic aspects of schizophrenic psychoses. *Proc. Tenth Intern. Congr. Genet.*, **1**, 81–8.

BRNCIC, D. and KOREF-SANTIBAÑEZ, S. 1964. Mating activity of homo- and heterokaryotypes in *Drosophila pavani*. *Genetics*, **49**, 585–91.

BROADHURST, P. L. 1960. Experiments in psychogenetics. Applications of biometrical genetics to the inheritance of behaviour. *Experiments in Personality*, Vol. I (ed. H. J. Eysenck), pp. 1–102. Routledge and Kegan Paul, London.

—— 1964. The hereditary base for the action of drugs on animal behaviour. *Ciba Foundation Symp.* on *'Animal behaviour and drug action'*, pp. 224–37.

—— and JINKS, J. L. 1961. Biometrical genetics and behaviour: Reanalysis of published data. *Psychol. Bulletin*, **58**, 337–62.

—— and JINKS, J. L. 1963. The inheritance of mammalian behavior re-examined. *J. Hered.*, **54**, 170–6.

—— and WATSON, R. H. J. 1964. Brain cholinesterase, body build and emotionality in different strains of rats. *Anim. Behaviour*, **12**, 42–51.

M

BRODY, E. G. 1942. Genetic basis of spontaneous activity in the albino rat. *Comp. Psychol. Monogr.*, **17**(5), 1–24.

BRUELL, J. H. 1962. Dominance and segregation in the inheritance of quantitative behavior in mice. In *Roots of Behavior* (ed. E. L. Bliss), pp. 48–67, Harper, New York.

—— 1964 *a*. Heterotic inheritance of wheelrunning in mice. *J. Comp. Physiol. Psychol.*, **58**, 159–63.

—— 1964 *b*. Inheritance of behavioral and physiological characters of mice and the problem of heterosis. *Am. Zoologist*, **4**, 125–38.

BURT, C. 1943. Ability and income. *Brit. J. Educ. Psychol.*, **13**, 83–98.

CAIN, A. J. and SHEPPARD, P. M. 1954. Natural selection in *Cepaea*. *Genetics*, **39**, 89–116.

CARMODY, G., COLLAZO, A. D., DOBZHANSKY, TH., EHRMAN, L., JAFFREY, I. S., KIMBALL, S., OBREBSKI, S., SILAGI, S., TIDWELL, T., and ULLRICH, R. 1962. Mating preferences and sexual isolation within and between the incipient species of *Drosophila paulistorum*. *Am. Midl. Nat.*, **68**, 67–82.

CARSON, H. L. 1951. Breeding sites of *Drosophila pseudoobscura* and *Drosophila persimilis* in the Transition zone of the Sierra Nevada. *Evolution*, **5**, 91–6.

—— 1958. Response to selection under different conditions of recombination in *Drosophila*. *Cold Spring Harbor Symp. Quant. Biol.*, **23**, 291–306.

CATTELL, R. B. 1953. Research designs in psychological genetics with special reference to the multiple variance method. *Amer. J. Human Genet.*, **5**, 76–93.

—— 1960. The multiple abstract variance analysis equations and solutions: for nature–nurture research on continuous variables. *Psychol. Review*, **67**, 353–72.

—— 1965. Methodological and conceptual advances in evaluating hereditary and environmental influences and their interaction. *Methods and goals in human behavior genetics* (ed. S. G. Vandenberg), pp. 95–139. Academic Press.

——, BLEWETT, D. B., and BELOFF, J. R. 1955. The inheritance of personality. A multiple variance analysis determination of approximate nature–nurture ratios for primary personality factors in Q-data. *Amer. J. Hum. Genet.*, **7**, 122–46.

CAVALLI, L. L. 1952. An analysis of linkage in quantitative inheritance. *Quantitative Inheritance* (eds. E. C. R. Reeve and C. H. Waddington), pp. 135–44. H.M.S.O., London.

CLARK, P. J. 1956. The heritability of certain anthropometric characters as ascertained from measurements of twins. *Amer. J. Hum. Genet.*, **8**, 49–54.

COLEMAN, D. L. 1960. Phenylalanine hydroxylase activity in dilute and nondilute strains of mice. *Arch. Biochem. Biophys.*, **91**, 300–6.

COLLINS, R. L. 1964. Inheritance of avoidance conditioning in mice: diallel study. *Science*, **143**, 1188–90.

COOCH, F. G. and BEARDMORE, J. A. 1959. Assortative mating and reciprocal difference in the Blue Snow Goose complex. *Nature*, **183**, 1833–4.

DAWSON, W. M. 1932. Inheritance of wildness and tameness in mice. *Genetics*, **17**, 296–326.

DETHIER, V. G. and STELLAR, E. 1961. *Animal Behavior: Its evolutionary and neurological basis.* Prentice-Hall, New Jersey.

DOBZHANSKY, TH. 1937. *Genetics and the Origin of Species* (1st edn). Columbia University Press.

—— 1944. Experiments on sexual isolation in *Drosophila*. III. Geographic strains of *Drosophila sturtevanti*. *Proc. Natl. Acad. Sci.*, *U.S.*, **30**, 335–9.

—— 1947 *a*. Adaptive changes induced by natural selection in wild populations of *Drosophila*. *Evolution*, **1**, 1–16.

—— 1947 *b*. Genetics of natural populations. XIV. A response of certain gene arrangements in the third chromosome of *Drosophila pseudoobscura* to natural selection. *Genetics*, **32**, 142–60.

—— 1948. Genetics of natural populations. XVI. Altitudinal and seasonal changes produced by natural selection in certain populations of *Drosophila pseudoobscura* and *Drosophila persimilis*. *Genetics*, **33**, 158–76.

—— 1951. *Genetics and the Origin of Species* (3rd edn). Columbia University Press.

—— 1955. A review of some fundamental concepts and problems of population genetics. *Cold Spring Harbor Symp. Quant. Biol.*, **20**, 1–15.

—— and LEVENE, H. 1955. Genetics of natural populations. XXIV. Developmental homeostasis in natural populations of *Drosophila pseudoobscura*. *Genetics*, **40**, 797–808.

—— and SPASSKY, B. 1959. *Drosophila paulistorum*, a cluster of species in statu nascendi. *Proc. Natl. Acad. Sci.*, *U.S.*, **45**, 419–28.

—— and SPASSKY, B. 1962. Selection for geotaxis in monomorphic and polymorphic populations of *Drosophila pseudoobscura*. *Proc. Natl. Acad. Sci.*, *U.S.*, **48**, 1704–12.

——, LEWONTIN, R. C., and PAVLOVSKY, O. 1964. The capacity for increase in chromosomally polymorphic and monomorphic populations of *Drosophila pseudoobscura*. *Heredity*, **19**, 597–614.

—— and MAYR, E. 1944. Experiments on sexual isolation in *Drosophila*. I. Geographic strains of *Drosophila willistoni*. *Proc. Natl. Acad. Sci.*, *U.S.*, **30**, 238–44.

DOBZHANSKY, TH. and STREISINGER, G. 1944. Experiments on sexual isolation in *Drosophila*. II. Geographic strains of *Drosophila prosaltans*. *Proc. Natl. Acad. Sci., U.S.*, **30**, 340–5.

DUNCAN, C. J. and SHEPPARD, P. M. 1965. Sensory discrimination and its role in the evolution of Batesian mimicry. *Behaviour*, **24**, 269–82.

EHRMAN, L. 1960. The genetics of hybrid sterility in *Drosophila paulistorum*. *Evolution*, **14**, 212–23.

—— 1961. The genetics of sexual isolation in *Drosophila paulistorum*. *Genetics*, **46**, 1025–38.

—— 1964 *a*. Courtship and mating behavior as a reproductive isolating mechanism in *Drosophila*. *Am. Zoologist*, **4**, 147–53.

—— 1964 *b*. Genetic divergence in M. Vetukhiv's experimental populations of *Drosophila pseudoobscura*. I. Rudiments of sexual isolation. *Genet. Res., Camb.*, **5**, 150–7.

—— 1965. Direct observation of sexual isolation between allopatric and between sympatric strains of the different *Drosophila paulistorum* races. *Evolution*, **19**, 459–64.

——, SPASSKY, B., PAVLOVSKY, O., and DOBZHANSKY, TH. 1965. Sexual selection, geotaxis, and chromosomal polymorphism in experimental populations of *Drosophila pseudoobscura*. *Evolution*, **19**, 337–46.

EIDUSON, S., GELLER, E., YUWILER, A., and EIDUSON, B. T. 1964. *Biochemistry and Behavior*. van Nostrand, Princeton.

ELENS, A. A. and WATTIAUX, J. M. 1964. Direct observation of sexual isolation. *Drosophila Information Service*, **39**, 118–19.

ERLENMEYER-KIMLING, L. and JARVIK, L. F. 1963. Genetics and intelligence: A review. *Science*, **142**, 1477–9.

EWING, A. W. 1964. The influence of wing area on the courtship behaviour of *Drosophila melanogaster*. *Amin. Behaviour*, **12**, 316–20.

EYSENCK, H. J. 1956. The inheritance of extraversion–introversion. *Acta. Psychologica*, **12**, 95–110.

—— and BROADHURST, P. L. 1964. Experiments with animals. Introduction. *Experiments in Motivation* (ed. H. J. Eysenck), pp. 285–91. Pergamon Press.

FALCONER, D. S. 1960. *Introduction to Quantitative Genetics*. Oliver and Boyd, Edinburgh.

FISCHER, R., GRIFFIN, F., ENGLAND, S., and GARN, S. M. 1961. Taste thresholds and food dislikes. *Nature*, **191**, 1328.

FISHER, R. A. 1918. The correlation between relatives on the supposition of Mendelian inheritance. *Trans. Roy. Soc. Edin.*, **52**, 399–433.

—— 1922. On the dominance ratio. *Proc. Roy. Soc. Edin.*, **42**, 321–41.

—— 1930. *The Genetical Theory of Natural Selection*. Clarendon Press, Oxford.

FISHER, R. A. 1949. A preliminary linkage test with agouti and undulated mice. *Heredity*, **3**, 229–41.

—— 1950. *Statistical Methods for Research Workers* (11th edn). Oliver and Boyd, Edinburgh.

FORD, E. B. 1964. *Ecological Genetics.* Methuen, London.

FULLER, J. L. 1964. Physiological and population aspects of behavior genetics. *Am. Zoologist*, **4**, 101–9.

—— and THOMPSON, W. R. 1960. *Behavior Genetics.* John Wiley, New York.

GIBSON, J. B. and THODAY, J. M. 1962. Effects of disruptive selection. VI. A second chromosome polymorphism. *Heredity*, **17**, 1–26.

GINSBURG, B. and ALLEE, W. C. 1942. Some effects of conditioning on social dominance and subordination in inbred strains of mice. *Physiol. Zool.*, **15**, 485–506.

GOY, R. W. and JAKWAY, J. S. 1959. The inheritance of patterns of sexual behaviour in female guinea pigs. *Anim. Behav.*, **7**, 142–9.

GRIFFING, B. 1956. Concept of general and specific combining ability in relation to diallel crossing systems. *Aust. J. Biol. Sci.*, **9**, 463–93.

HALL, C. S. 1951. The genetics of behavior. *Handbook of Experimental Psychology* (ed. S. S. Stevens), pp. 304–29. John Wiley, New York.

HATT, D. and PARSONS, P. A. 1965. Association between surnames and blood groups in the Australian population. *Acta Genetica*, **15**, 309–18.

HAYMAN, B. I. 1958. The theory and analysis of diallel crosses. II. *Genetics*, **43**, 63–85.

HIRSCH, J. 1962. Individual differences in behavior and their genetic basis. *Roots of Behavior* (ed. E. L. Bliss), pp. 3–23. Harper, New York.

—— 1963. Behavior genetics and individuality understood. *Science*, **142**, 1436–42.

HOLZINGER, K. J. 1929. The relative effect of nature and nurture influences on twin differences. *J. Educ. Psychol.*, **20**, 241–8.

HSIA, D. Y-Y. 1959. *Inborn Errors of Metabolism.* Year Book Publishers, Chicago.

HUXLEY, J., MAYR, E., OSMOND, H., and HOFFER, A. 1964. Schizophrenia as a genetic morphism. *Nature*, **204**, 220–1.

JAKWAY, J. S. 1959. Inheritance of patterns of mating behaviour in the male guinea pig. *Anim. Behav.*, **7**, 150–62.

KALMUS, H. 1949. Tone deafness and its inheritance. Proc. 8th Int. Congr. Genetics, Stockholm. *Hereditas*, Supplementary vol. p. 605.

KALOW, W. 1962. *Pharmacogenetics: heredity and the response to drugs.* W. B. Saunders, Philadelphia.

KAUL, D. and PARSONS, P. A. 1965. The genotypic control of mating speed and duration of copulation in *Drosophila pseudoobscura*. *Heredity*, **20**, 381–92.

164   THE GENETIC ANALYSIS OF BEHAVIOUR

KEMPTHORNE, O. 1957. *An Introduction to Genetic Statistics.* John Wiley, New York.

KETTLEWELL, H. B. D. 1956. Further selection experiments on industrial melanism in the Lepidoptera. *Heredity,* **10**, 287–301.

KNIGHT, G. R., ROBERTSON, A., and WADDINGTON, C. H. 1956. Selection for sexual isolation within a species. *Evolution,* **10**, 14–22.

KOOPMAN, K. F. 1950. Natural selection for reproductive isolation between *Drosophila pseudoobscura* and *Drosophila persimilis. Evolution,* **4**, 135–48.

KOREF-SANTIBAÑEZ, S. 1964. Reproductive isolation between the sibling species *Drosophila pavani* and *Drosophila gaucha. Evolution,* **18**, 245–51.

—— and WADDINGTON, C. H. 1958. The origin of sexual isolation between different lines within a species. *Evolution,* **12**, 485–93.

LANGRIDGE, J. 1962. A genetic and molecular basis for heterosis in *Arabidopsis* and *Drosophila. Am. Naturalist,* **96**, 5–27.

LERNER, I. M. 1954. *Genetic Homeostasis.* Oliver and Boyd, Edinburgh.

LEVENE, H. 1949. A new measure of sexual isolation. *Evolution,* **3**, 315–21.

LEVINE, L. 1958. Studies on sexual selection in mice. I. Reproductive competition between albino and black-agouti males. *Am. Naturalist,* **92**, 21–6.

——, BARSEL, G. E., and DIAKOW, C. A. 1965. Interaction of aggressive and sexual behavior in male mice. *Behaviour,* **26**, 272–80.

—— and LASCHER, B. 1965. Studies on sexual selection in mice. II. Reproductive competition between black and brown males. *Am. Naturalist,* **99**, 67–72.

LI, C. C. 1961. *Human Genetics: Principles and Methods.* McGraw-Hill, New York.

LYON, M. F. 1962. Sex chromatin and gene action in the mammalian X-chromosome. *Amer. J. Hum. Genet.,* **14**, 135–48.

MAAS, J. W. 1963. Neurochemical differences between two strains of mice. *Nature,* **197**, 255–7.

MACBEAN, I. T. and PARSONS, P. A. 1966. The genotypic control of the duration of copulation in *Drosophila melanogaster. Experientia,* **22**, 101–2.

MCCLEARN, G. E. 1961. Genotype and mouse activity. *J. Comp. Physiol. Psychol.,* **54**, 674–6.

——, BENNETT, E. L., HEBERT, M., KAKIHANA, R., and SCHLESINGER, K. 1964. Alcohol dehydrogenase activity and previous ethanol consumption in mice. *Nature,* **203**, 793–4.

MCGILL, T. E. and BLIGHT, W. C. 1963. The sexual behaviour of hybrid male mice compared with the sexual behaviour of males of the inbred parent strains. *Anim. Behaviour,* **11**, 480–3.

MCKUSICK, V. A. 1964. *Human Genetics*. Prentice-Hall, New Jersey.

MAINARDI, D., MARSAN, M., and PASQUALI, A. 1965 *a*. Causation of sexual preferences of the house mouse. The behaviour of mice reared by parents whose odour was artificially altered. *Atti della Società Italiana di Scienze Naturali e del Museo Civico di Storia Naturali di Milano*, **104**, 325–38.

MAINARDI, D., MARSAN, M., and PASQUALI, A. 1965 *b*. Assenza di preferenze sessuali tra ceppi nel maschio di *Mus musculus domesticus*. *Istituto Lombardo (Rend Sc.)*, **99**, 26–34.

MALOGOLOWKIN-COHEN, C. H., SIMMONS, A. S., and LEVENE, H. 1965. A study of sexual isolation between certain strains of *Drosophila paulistorum*. *Evolution*, **19**, 95–103.

MANNING, A. 1961. The effects of artificial selection for mating speed in *Drosophila melanogaster*. *Anim. Behaviour*, **9**, 82–92.

—— 1963. Selection for mating speed in *Drosophila melanogaster* based on the behaviour of one sex. *Anim. Behaviour*, **11**, 116–20.

MATHER, K. 1942. The balance of polygenic combinations. *J. Genet.*, **43**, 309–36.

—— 1943. Polygenic inheritance and natural selection. *Biol. Rev.*, **18**, 32–64.

—— 1949. *Biometrical Genetics*. Methuen, London.

—— 1955. Polymorphism as an outcome of disruptive selection. *Evolution*, **9**, 52–61.

—— and HARRISON, B. J. 1949. The manifold effect of selection. *Heredity*, **3**, 1–52, 131–62.

MAYNARD SMITH, J. 1962. Disruptive selection, polymorphism and sympatric speciation. *Nature*, **195**, 60–2.

MAYR, E. 1963. *Animal Species and Evolution*. Harvard University Press.

—— and DOBZHANSKY, TH. 1945. Experiments on sexual isolation in *Drosophila*. IV. Modification of the degree of isolation between *Drosophila pseudoobscura* and *Drosophila persimilis* and of sexual preferences in *Drosophila prosaltans*. *Proc. Natl. Acad. Sci., U.S.*, **31**, 75–82.

MEDAWAR, P. B. 1957. *The Uniqueness of the Individual*. Methuen London.

MEIER, H. 1963. *Experimental Pharmacogenetics, Physiopathology of Heredity, and Pharmacologic Responses*. Academic Press, New York.

MERRELL, D. J. 1949. Selective mating in *Drosophila melanogaster*. *Genetics*, **34**, 370–89.

—— 1953. Selective mating as a cause of gene frequency changes in laboratory populations of *Drosophila melanogaster*. *Evolution*, **7**, 287–96.

MILKMAN, R. D. 1962. The genetic basis of natural variation. IV. On the natural distribution of *cve* polygenes of *Drosophila melanogaster*. *Genetics*, **47**, 261–72.

NEEL, J. V. and SCHULL, W. J. 1954. *Human Heredity*. University of Chicago Press.

NEWMAN, H. H., FREEMAN, F. N., and HOLZINGER, K. J. 1937. *Twins: a study of heredity and environment*. University of Chicago Press.

O'DONALD, P. 1959. Possibility of assortive mating in the Artic Skua. *Nature*, **183**, 1210–11.

—— 1960. Assortive mating in a population in which two alleles are segregating. *Heredity*, **15**, 389–96.

PARSONS, P. A. 1959. Genotypic–environmental interactions for various temperatures in *Drosophila melanogaster*. *Genetics*, **44**, 1325–33.

—— 1961. Fly size, emergence time and sternopleural chaeta number in *Drosophila*. *Heredity*, **16**, 455–73.

—— 1962. The initial increase of a new gene under positive assortative mating. *Heredity*, **17**, 267–76.

—— 1964. A diallel cross for mating speeds in *Drosophila melanogaster*. *Genetica*, **35**, 141–51.

—— 1965 *a*. The determination of mating speeds in *Drosophila melanogaster* for various combinations of inbred lines. *Experientia*, **21**, 478.

—— 1965 *b*. Assortative mating for a metrical characteristic in *Drosophila*. *Heredity*, **20**, 161–7.

—— and KAUL, D. 1966 *a*. Mating speed and duration of copulation in *Drosophila pseudoobscura*. *Heredity*, **21**, 219–25.

—— and KAUL, D. 1967. Variability within and between strains for mating behaviour parameters in *Drosophila pseudoobscura*. *Experientia*, **23**, 131–2.

PEARSON, K. and LEE, A. 1903. On the laws of inheritance in man. I. Inheritance of physical characters. *Biometrika*, **2**, 357–462.

PENROSE, L. S. 1963. *The Biology of Mental Defect* (3rd edn). Sidgwick and Jackson, London.

PETIT, C. 1959. La déterminisme génétique et psycho-physiologique de la compétition sexuelle chez *Drosophila melanogaster*. *Bull. Biol. France Belgique*, **92**, 248–329.

PITTENDRIGH, C. S. 1958. Adaptation, natural selection, and behavior. *Behavior and Evolution* (eds. A. Roe, and G. G. Simpson), pp. 390–416. Yale University Press.

RENDEL, J. M. 1951. Mating of ebony vestigial and wild-type *Drosophila melanogaster* in light and dark. *Evolution*, **5**, 226–30.

ROBERTS, J. A. F. 1952. The genetics of mental deficiency. *Eugen. Rev.*, **44**, 71–83.

RODGERS, D. A. and MCCLEARN, G. E. 1962 *a*. Mouse strain differences in preference for various concentrations of alcohol. *Quart. J. Studies on Alcohol*, **23**, 26–33.

RODGERS, D. A. and MCCLEARN, G. E. 1962 *b*. Alcohol preference of mice. *Roots of Behavior* (ed. E. L. Bliss), pp. 68–95. Harper, New York.

RODGERS, D. A., MCCLEARN, G. E., BENNETT, E. L., and HEBERT, M. 1963. Alcohol preference as a function of its caloric utility in mice. *J. Comp. Physiol. Psychol.*, **56**, 666–72.

RUNDQUIST, E. A. 1933. Inheritance of spontaneous activity in rats. *J. Comp. Psychol.*, **16**, 415–38.

SCOTT, J. P. and FREDERICSON, E. 1951. The causes of fighting in mice and rats. *Physiol. Zool.*, **24**, 273–309.

SHEPPARD, P. M. 1963. Mimicry and its ecological aspects. *Genetics Today*, Vol. 3 (*Proc. XI International Congress of Genetics*), pp. 553–60.

SIDMAN, R. L., APPEL, S. H., and FULLER, J. L. 1965. Neurological mutants of the mouse. *Science*, **150**, 513–16.

SLATER, E. 1958. The monogenic theory of schizophrenia. *Acta. Genet.*, **8**, 50–6.

SNYDER, L. H. 1932. Studies in human inheritance. IX. The inheritance of taste deficiency in man. *Ohio. J. Sci.*, **32**, 436–40.

SPIESS, E. B. and LANGER, B. 1961. Chromosomal adaptive polymorphism in *Drosophila persimilis*. III. Mating propensity of homokaryotypes. *Evolution*, **15**, 535–44.

SPIESS, E. B. and LANGER, B. 1964 *a*. Mating speed control by gene arrangements in *Drosophila pseudoobscura* homokaryotypes. *Proc. Natl. Acad. Sci., U.S.*, **51**, 1015–19.

SPIESS, E. B. and LANGER, B. 1964 *b*. Mating speed control by gene arrangement carriers in *Drosophila persimilis*. *Evolution*, **18**, 430–44.

SPIESS, E. B., LANGER, B., and SPIESS, L. D. 1966. Heterogamic mating control by gene arrangements in *Drosophila pseudoobscura*. *Genetics*, **54**, 1139–49.

SPIETH, H. T. 1958. Behavior and isolating mechanisms. *Behavior and Evolution* (eds. A. Roe and G. G. Simpson), pp. 363–89. Yale University Press.

STALKER, H. D. 1942. Sexual isolation studies in the species complex *Drosophila virilis*. *Genetics*, **27**, 238–57.

SPUHLER, J. N. 1962. Empirical studies on quantitative human genetics. *U.N./W.H.O. Seminar on 'The use of vital and health statistics for genetic and radiation studies'*, pp. 241–52.

STERN, C. 1960. *Principles of Human Genetics* (2nd edn). Freeman, San Francisco.

STURTEVANT, A. H. 1915. Experiments on sex recognition and the problem of sexual selection in *Drosophila*. *J. Anim. Behav.*, 5, 351–66.

—— 1929. The genetics of *Drosophila simulans*. *Carnegie Inst. Wash. Publ.*, 399, 1–62.

THODAY, J. M. 1961. Location of polygenes. *Nature*, 191, 368–70.

—— 1964. Genetics and the integration of reproductive systems. *Insect Reproduction* (ed. K. C. Highnam), *Symp. No. 2. Royal. Ent. Soc.*, pp. 108–19.

—— and BOAM, T. B. 1961. Regular responses to selection. I. Description of responses. *Genetic. Res.*, Camb., 2, 161–76.

——, GIBSON, J. B., and SPICKETT, S. G. 1963. Some polygenes. *Heredity*, 18, 553–4.

TRYON, R. C. 1942. Individual differences. *Comparative psychology* (2nd edn) (ed. F. A. Moss), pp. 330–65. Prentice-Hall, New York.

VICARI, E. M. 1929. Mode of inheritance of reaction time and degrees of learning in mice. *J. Exp. Zool.*, 54, 31–88.

VILLEE, C. A. 1964. *Biology* (4th edn). W. B. Saunders Company, Philadelphia.

WALLACE, B. 1954. Genetic divergence of isolated populations of *Drosophila melanogaster*. *Caryologia*, Vol. 6, Suppl., pp. 761–4.

WEARDEN, S. 1964. Alternative analyses of the diallel cross. *Heredity*, 19, 669–80.

WILLIAMS, R. J. 1956. *Biochemical Individuality*. John Wiley, New York.

WOLSTENHOLME, D. R. and THODAY, J. M. 1963. Effects of disruptive selection. VII. A third chromosome polymorphism. *Heredity*, 18, 413–31.

WOOLLEY, D. W. and VAN DER HOEVEN, TH. 1963. Alteration in learning ability caused by changes in cerebral serotonin and catechol amines. *Science*, 139, 610–11.

WRIGHT, S. 1921. Systems of mating. *Genetics*, 6, 111–78.

—— and DOBZHANSKY, TH. 1946. Genetics of natural populations. XII. Experimental reproduction of some of the changes caused by natural selection in certain populations of *Drosophila pseudoobscura*. *Genetics*, 31, 125–50.

Index

Acquired behaviour, 4
Acrocephaly, 126
Activity
  in *Drosophila*, 69, 70
  in mice, 104-5
  in rats, 44, 60, 62-3, 104
Adopted children, 143
Alcohol consumption in mice, 113-16
Alcohol dehydrogenase, 115-16
Allee, W. C., 106, 163
Allopatric species, 90-1, 95, 101
Anencephaly, 131
Appel, S. H., 103, 118, 167
Aromatic amino acids, 116-19
Assortative mating, 54, 85
  in *Drosophila* strains, 98-100, 102
  in man, 148-51
Audiogenic seizures, 105-6
  in mice, 60, 106, 118
  in rats, 60, 106
Auditory discrimination, 148

Balanced genotype, 153
Barker, J. S. F., 94, 159
Barsel, G. E., 108, 164
Bastock, M., 7-10, 159
Bateman, A. J., 85, 159
Beardmore, J. A., 11, 99, 159, 161
Beckman, L., 150-1, 159
Beloff, J. R., 144, 160
Bennett, E. L., 164, 167
Bignami, G., 111, 159
Biometrical methods, 2-3, 26-56, 62, 75, 132-7
Birch, L. C., 12, 159

Biston, 22
Blair, W. F., 109
Blewett, D. B., 144, 160
Blight, W. C., 105, 165
Boam, T. B., 59, 168
Böök, J. A., 139, 159
Brncic, D., 21, 159
Broadhurst, P. L., 40, 42-4, 60-3, 103-6, 110-12, 119-20, 159, 162
Brody, E. G., 60, 104, 160
Bruell, J. H., 39, 104-5, 160
Burt, C., 143, 160

Cain, A. J., 24, 160
Carmody, G., 90-2, 160
Carson, H. L., 67-8, 94, 160
Cattell, R. B., 132, 136-7, 144, 160
Cavalli, L. L., 40, 42, 160
Cepaea nemoralis, 24
Chaeta number in *Drosophila*, 59, 71-4, 98-100
Choice experiments
  in *Drosophila*, 79-83
  in mice, 107-9
Cholinesterase, 119-20
Clark, P. J., 149, 161
Clarke, C. A., 23
Coadapted complex, 153-5
Coefficient of isolation, 84
Coefficient of sexual isolation, 86
Coleman, D. L., 118, 161
Collazo, A. D., 160
Collins, R. L., 111, 161
Colour blindness, 129, 146-8
Conrad, K., 138

Cooch, F. G., 99, 161
Copulation duration in Drosophila, 16–17, 32–4, 51, 155
Correlation between relatives, 52–6, 136, 142
Courtship in Drosophila, 8–10, 78
Covariance
between genotype and environment, 31, 40–1
between relatives, 52–3, 136

Darwin, C., 85
Dawson, W. M., 42, 106, 161
Defecation in rats, 44, 60–3, 106
Density–dependent mating in Drosophila, 19, 88
Dethier, V. G., 4, 161
Diakow, C. A., 108, 164
Diallel cross, 43–51, 55, 60, 62
Disruptive (diversifying) selection, 73–4, 98–9
Dobzhansky, Th., 11–12, 51, 67, 77–8, 89–91, 94–5, 153–5, 159–62, 165, 168
Down's syndrome, 123–5, 133
Drosophila, 3–6, 30, 55–6, 62, 64, 93, 102, 120, 154–5, 157
activity, 69–70
copulation duration, 16–17, 32–4, 51, 155
courtship, 8–10, 78
gaucha, 21, 95, 101
geotaxis, 64–7
learning, 94
mating behaviour, 7–11, 15–22
mating speed, 15–21, 44–51, 68–70, 155
melanogaster, 7–10, 32–4, 44–51, 59, 64–76, 82, 86–9, 94, 156
motility, 67
paulistorum, 90–3, 101
pavani, 21, 95, 101
persimilis, 11, 19–21, 82, 93–5, 156

Drosophila, (contd.)
phototaxis, 67, 82, 156
prosaltans, 89, 90
pseudoobscura, 11–12, 14–19, 49–51, 67, 70, 82–3, 88, 93–8, 154, 156
races, 89–93
robusta, 67
simulans, 94, 156
strains, 89–93
sturtevanti, 89–90
willistoni, 89–90
Drugs in mice and rats, 120
Duncan, C. J., 24, 162
Duration of copulation (see Copulation)
Dystrophia myotonica, 126

Early experience, 30, 107, 113, 120
Ehrman, L., 18, 78, 81, 84, 91, 96–8, 160, 162
Eiduson, B. T., 162
Eiduson, S., 113, 129, 162
Elens, A. A., 80–1, 91, 162
Emotionality
in mice, 106
in rats, 106, 112
England, S., 162
Environment
intelligence, 142–4
interaction with genotype, 31, 34–6, 41, 51, 55, 135–7, 144
multiple, 34–6, 55, 83, 93–4
temperature, 51, 156
Epilepsy, 131, 138
Epiloia, 126
Epistasis, 37–8, 40–1, 43
Equilibrium, 11–14
Erlenmeyer-Kimling, L., 65, 67, 142, 162
Ethological isolation, 77–8, 93–4
Evolutionary change, 157–8
Ewing, A. W., 100, 162
Experience, 107, 113

Exploration in mice, 104–5
Eysenck, H. J., 112, 145, 162

Falconer, D. S., 30, 41, 52, 58–9, 103, 162
Fighting in mice, 106–7
Fischer, R., 146–7, 162
Fisher, R. A., 11, 23, 30, 46, 99, 134, 149, 162–3
Fitness, 13, 14, 51, 59, 98, 112, 153–4
Ford, E. B., 22–4, 163
Fredericson, E., 107, 167
Freeman, F. N., 135, 166
Fuller, J. L., 103–6, 109, 111, 118–19, 138–9, 148, 163, 167

Galactosaemia, 129–30
Galton, F., 53
Garn, S. M., 162
Gedda, L., 133
Geller, E., 162
General combining ability, 47–9
Genes affecting behaviour
    in Drosophila, 7–11, 66–7, 86–9
    in man, 125–31
    in mice, 103, 118
    in rats, 60
Genetic individuality, 1
Genotypic value, 28–31, 36–9
Geotaxis in Drosophila, 64–7
Gibson, J. B., 73–4, 98, 163, 168
Ginsburg, B., 106, 163
Goy, R. W., 105, 163
Griffin, F., 162
Griffing, B., 44, 46, 48, 163
Guinea pigs – sexual behaviour, 105

Hall, C. S., 106, 163
Harrison, B. J., 65, 96, 165
Hatt, D., 151, 163
Hayman, B. I., 44, 163
Hebert, M., 164, 167
Heterosis, 45–6, 104–5, 111–12

Heritability, 56, 75
    in the broad sense, 34, 36
    in the narrow sense, 38, 52–4, 57–8
    in twin data, 133–4
Hirsch, J., 64–7, 163
Hoffer, A., 163
Holzinger, K. J., 134–5, 163, 166
Homeostasis
    behavioural, 51, 156
    developmental, 154, 156
    genetic, 155
Hosgood, S. M. W., 70, 156
Howard, W. E., 109
Hsia, D. Y.-Y., 129, 163
Huntingdon's chorea, 125–6
Huxley, J., 140, 163
Hybrid sterility, 78, 90–2
Hybrid vigour (see Heterosis)
Hydrocephaly, 129, 131

Imprinting, 109, 151
Inbred strains, 3, 31–6
    crosses between, 38–49, 55–6
Industrial melanism, 22, 25
Innate behaviour, 4, 94
Intelligence, 122, 137, 141–5
    assortative mating, 150
Introversion–extroversion factor, 145
Inversions – behavioural effects, 15–22, 49–51, 67
I.Q. test, 141–4
Isolating mechanism, 77–8, 90
Isolation index, 83, 91–2

Jaffrey, I. S., 160
Jakway, J. S., 105, 163
Jarvik, L. F., 142, 162
Jinks, J. L., 40, 42–3, 104–6, 110–11, 159

Kakihana, R., 164
Kalmus, H., 148, 163
Kalow, W., 130, 163
Karyotype abnormalities, 123–5

Kaul, D., 16–18, 50–1, 155, 164, 166
Kempthorne, O., 30, 44, 164
Kettlewell, H. B. D., 22, 164
Kimball, S., 160
Klinefelter's syndrome, 124–5
Knight, G. R., 96, 164
Koopman, K. F., 95, 164
Koref-Santibañez, S., 21, 95–6, 159, 164

Langer, B., 15, 16, 18–21, 83, 167
Langridge, J., 51, 164
Lascher, B., 107, 164
Leahy, A. M., 143
Learning, 5, 120
  in Drosophila, 94
  in mice, 109–11, 118–19
  in rats, 111
Lee, A., 149, 166
Lepidoptera, 6, 22–3
Lerner, I. M., 155, 164
Levene, H., 51, 84, 155, 161, 164–5
Levine, L., 107–8, 164
Lewontin, R. C., 11, 161
Li, C. C., 127, 164
Location of polygenes, 71–5
Lyon, M. F., 124, 164

Maas, J. W., 119, 164
MacBean, I. T., 32, 70, 164
Mainardi, D., 108–9, 165
Major gene, 29, 75
Malogolowkin-Cohen, C. H., 84, 165
Man, 3–5, 52–6, 99, 117–19, 122–52, 157–8
Manic depressive psychosis, 131, 141
Manning, A., 68–70, 165
Marsan, M., 108–9, 165
Maternal age, 123
Mather, K., 30, 39, 44, 65, 71, 75, 96, 98, 153, 165

Mating behaviour
  in Drosophila, 7–22, 77–102
  in rats, 60
Mating chamber
  for Drosophila, 80–2, 91, 99
  for mice, 108
Mating speed in Drosophila, 15–21, 44–51, 68–70
MAVA method, 136–7, 144–5, 151
Maynard Smith, J., 98, 165
Mayr, E., 77–8, 89, 95, 98, 157–8, 162–3, 165
Maze learning
  in mice, 110–11
  in rats, 60, 111
Medawar, P. B., 1, 165
Meier, H., 113, 119–20, 165
Mental defect, 122–3, 125–7, 129–31, 137, 144
Mental illness, 137–41
Merrell, D. J., 87–8, 165–6
Metabolic disorders in man, 129–30
  treatment, 130
McClearn, G. E., 104, 113–16, 164, 167
McGill, T. E., 105, 165
McKusick, V. A., 130, 165
Milkman, R. D., 75, 166
Mice
  activity, 104–5
  alcohol consumption, 113–16
  audiogenic seizures, 60, 106, 118
  drugs, 120
  emotionality, 106
  exploration, 104–5
  fighting, 106–7
  learning, 109–11, 118–19
  maze learning, 110–11
  running speed, 42, 60
  sexual behaviour, 105, 107–9
  single genes, 103
  sub-species bactrianus, 109
  wildness, 42, 106

Mimicry, 22–5
  Batesian, 23–4
  Müllerian, 22–3
Multiple abstract variance analysis (see MAVA method)
Muscular dystrophy, 129

Neel, J. V., 126, 133–5, 166
Neurofibromatosis, 126
Newman, H. H., 135, 166
Normal distribution, 26–8

Obrebski, S., 160
O'Donald, P., 99, 149, 166
Olfactory stimuli, 148
Osmond, H., 163

Papilio dardanus, 23–4, 154
Parsons, P. A., 16–18, 32, 44–5, 50–1, 70, 99, 100, 149, 151, 155–6, 163–4, 166
Pasquali, A., 108–9, 165
Pavlovsky, O. A., 11, 159, 161–2
Pearson, K., 54, 149, 166
Penrose, L. S., 123–4, 126–7, 137, 144, 166
Peromyscus, 109
Personality, 137, 145
Petit, C., 86, 88–9, 166
Phenocopy, 131
Phenotypic value, 30–1
Phenylalanine hydroxylase, 118
Phenylalanine metabolism, 117–19
Phenylketonuria, 117–19, 127, 131
Phototaxis in Drosophila, 67, 82, 156
Pittendrigh, C. S., 82–3, 156, 166
Polygene, 29–30, 71–5, 153
Polymorphism, 6, 11–14, 21–5, 98, 140, 146–8
Porphyria, 129–30
Predators, 6, 22–5

Previous experience (see Early experience)

Quantitative traits, 1–5, 26–60
  in Drosophila, 32–4, 44–51
  in man, 132–7
  in rodents, 104–13

Random mating, 12–13, 52, 54, 148
Rats
  activity, 44, 60, 62–3, 104
  audiogenic seizures, 60, 106
  cholinesterase, 119–20
  defecation, 44, 60–3, 106,
  drugs, 120
  emotionality, 106, 112
  learning, 111
  mating behaviour, 60
  maze learning, 60, 111
  sexual behaviour, 60
Raven, J. C., 150
Recombination, 71–3, 75
Regression – parent–offspring, 53–4, 143–4
Relationship between relatives, 52–6, 136, 142–4
Rendel, J. M., 89, 167
Roberts, J. A. F., 144, 167
Robertson, A., 96, 164
Rodents (see also Guinea pigs, Mice, Rats), 3–5, 30–1, 103–21, 157
Rodgers, D. A., 113–16, 167
Rundquist, E. A., 104, 167
Running speed in mice, 42, 60

Scales, 39–43
Schizophrenia, 131, 138–41
Schlesinger, K., 164
Schull, W. J., 126, 133–5, 166
Scott, J. P., 107, 167
Selection, 3, 57–76, 155
  accelerated responses, 59, 75
  differential, 57–8

Selection, (contd.)
  responses, 57–60
  sexual isolation, 95–9
Sense perception, 145–8
Serotonin, 118–19
Sex-chromosomes, 124–5
Sexual behaviour
  in guinea pigs, 105
  in mice, 105, 107–9
  in rats, 60
Sexual isolation, 77–102
  by selection, 95–9
  Drosophila species, 93–5
  Drosophila strains, 89–93
Sexual selection, 85–93
  Drosophila genes, 86–9
  Drosophila strains, 89–93
  mice, 107–9
Sheppard, P. M., 23–4, 154, 160, 162, 167
Sibling species, 93–5, 101, 155–6
Sibs, 52–3, 55, 136
Sidman, R. L., 103, 118, 167
Silagi, S., 160
Simmons, A. S., 165
Slater, E., 139, 167
Snyder, L. H., 127–9, 167
Spassky, B., 67, 91, 155, 161–2
Specific combining ability, 47–50
Spiess, E. B., 15, 16, 18–21, 83, 167
Spiess, L. D., 18, 167
Spieth, H. T., 93–4, 167
Spickett, S. G., 73, 168
Spina bifida, 131, 133
Spuhler, J. N., 149–50, 167
Stalker, H. D., 83, 167
Stellar, E., 4, 161
Stern, C., 135, 138, 141, 143, 168
Streisinger, G., 89, 162
Sturtevant, A. H., 7, 86–7, 94, 156, 168
Sympatric species, 77, 91, 93, 95, 101

Taste stimuli, 145–7
Taster trait, 127–9, 145–6
Temperature
  tolerances, 156
  variations, 51
Thoday, J. M., 59, 71, 73–5, 98–9, 163, 168
Thompson, W. R., 103–6, 111, 138–9, 148, 163
Tidwell, T., 160
Transformation, 28, 39, 40
  angular, 41, 46
  logarithmic, 41–2
Tryon, R. C., 111, 120, 168
Turner's syndrome, 124
Twin studies, 3, 4, 52–3, 55, 132–7

Ullrich, R., 160

van der Hoeven, Th., 119, 168
Variance
  additive genetic, 37–8
  definition, 28
  dominance, 37–8
  environmental, 31, 33–4
  epistatic, 37–8
  genotypic, 31, 33–4
  phenotypic, 31, 34
Vicari, E. M., 110, 168
Villee, C. A., 27, 168

Waddington, C. H., 96, 164
Wallace, B., 95, 168
Watson, R. H. J., 120, 159
Wattiaux, J. M., 80–1, 91, 162
Wearden, S., 44, 50, 168
Wildness in mice, 42, 106
Williams, R. J., 1, 168
Wolstenholme, D. R., 74, 168
Woolley, D. W., 119, 168
Wright, S., 11, 30, 168

Yuwiler, A., 162